For Sandra
The most gifted
'quilter' around!

With Our Love
Rick + Lesley

Christmas '93

CREATIVE QUILTING

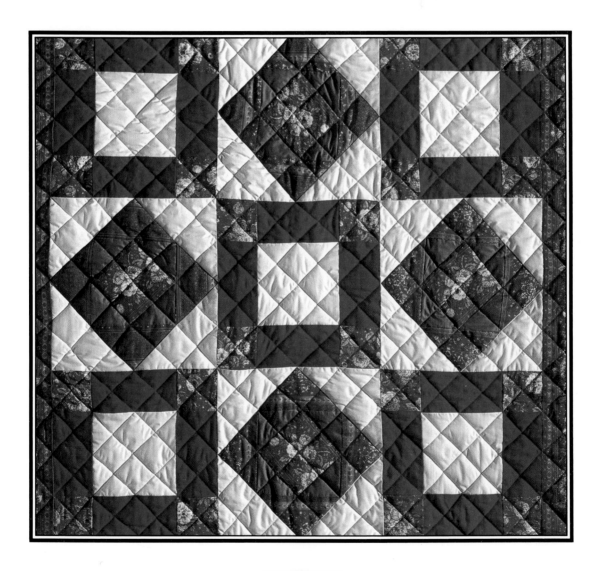

CHARTWELL
BOOKS, INC.

Contents

The Quilt Story   6

A Treasury of Quilts   8

The Quilter's Cupboard   12

Material Matters   14

Quilting Skills   16

Appliqué Quilts   20

Traditional Quilts   22

Log Cabin Quilts   24

Create a Quilt   26

Single Irish Chain   30

Tied Patches   36

Bits and Pieces   38

Ohio Stars   42

Basket Quilt   48

Square-in-Square   52

Triangle Wall Quilt   56

Flying Geese   60

Evening Star   64

Garden Path   72

Seminole Mountain   78

Scrap Bag Quilt   82

Pieces of Pie   88

Quick Quilts   92

Silk Nursery Quilt   94

Magic Quilt   100

Pillow Quilt   102

Patchwork Nursery
    Quilt   104

Chicken Wall Quilt   106

Quilted Cushions   110

Craft Editor: Tonia Todman
Managing Editor: Judy Poulos
Editorial Consultant: Beryl Hodges
Editorial Coordinator: Margaret Kelly
Production Manager: Sheridan Carter
Layout: Lulu Dougherty
Finished Art: Stephen Joseph
Illustrations: Lesley Griffith
Photography: Harm Mol, Andrew Elton,
Andrew Payne

Published by Chartwell Books, Inc.
A division of BOOKSALES, INC.
110 Enterprise Avenue
Secaucus, New Jersey 07094

Some of the contents of this book have been
previously published in other J.B. Fairfax Press
publications. All care has been taken to ensure
the accuracy of the information in this book
but no responsibility is accepted for any errors
or omissions.

ISBN 1 55521 850 4

Formatted by J.B. Fairfax Press Pty Limited
Printed by Toppan Printing Co, Singapore
PRINTED IN SINGAPORE

Foreword

The charm of an old patchwork quilt can't be explained by the sum of its parts. Whether it is a simple pattern of large squares sewn and tied, or a masterpiece of tiny pieces with beautiful quilting, the quilt has a special appeal because it is a unique piece of work, at once decorative and useful and often made with the heart as well as the hands. In a materialistic world, it also has the appeal of something that money can't buy.

The earliest patchwork quilts were made by frugal, rural women who stitched utilitarian bed covers from saved pieces of worn-out garments, or scraps from other projects. Later, mill workers in Britain, North America and Australia used samples from woolen mills. Sometimes these quilts were roughly sewn, but usually with an eye to the pleasing effect produced by placing one color or tone against another one.

Ladies of greater means saved precious pieces of special fabrics – chintzes, silks and satins, to make beautiful appliqué, pieced and crazy patchwork quilts.

The mosaic type of patchwork is probably the earliest style, developing an allover effect from simple templates, such as hexagons, which were often pieced over papers. The medallion style, which was built up around the central square, was common in England.

In America, the method of sewing together pieced blocks became a sophisticated folk art. The early pieced patterns, such as Log Cabin and Star of Bethlehem, which crossed the Atlantic with early settlers, were adapted and new designs flourished. The revival of interest in quiltmaking, especially since the United States Bicentenary, has been remarkable and reflects a new appreciation of traditional skills.

The making of a quilt needs only simple sewing skills – a running stitch for hand-piecing and hand-quilting, slipstitch for hemming and appliqué and a straight machine stitch for piecing blocks and sewing on bindings. It is a help to have a good eye for straight lines, or at least some respect for the grain of the fabric.

The art in quiltmaking lies in choosing a design and fabrics that are complementary and pleasing. Spend the time to consider these elements before starting. There is something very satisfying in completing a quilt, not the least of which is that it will last. A simple design of squares, machine-pieced and tied is quick to make and will add visual delight to a room. A complex design, with lots of fine hand-quilting may take a long time to make, but it will have an heirloom quality that a mass-produced bedcover can never imitate. An added bonus to the quilter is the time it allows to contemplate while quilting – a wonderful luxury in a busy world.

Margot Child

The Quilt
Story

*Q*uilting is both an art, rich in creativity, and a craft with all the pleasures of working on a project with skill and quiet enjoyment.

A TREASURY OF QUILTS

Choy-Lin Williams

Lesley Simpson

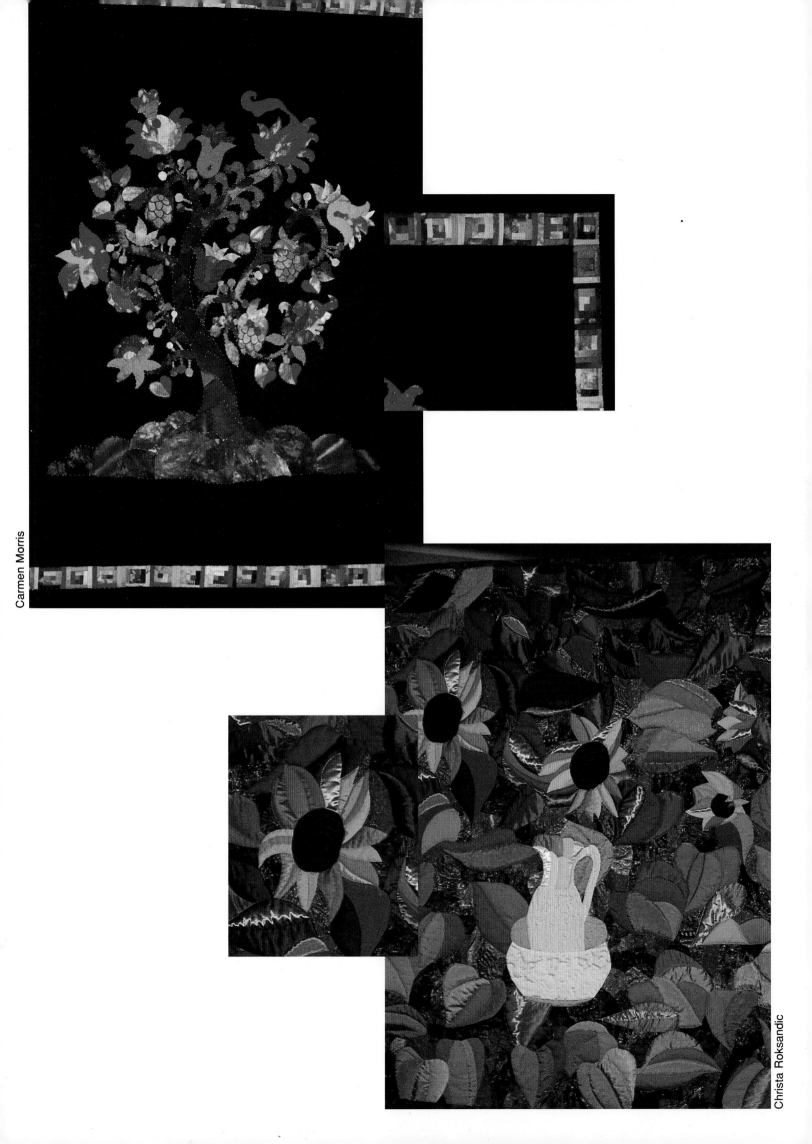

Carmen Morris

Christa Roksandic

Anne Whitsed

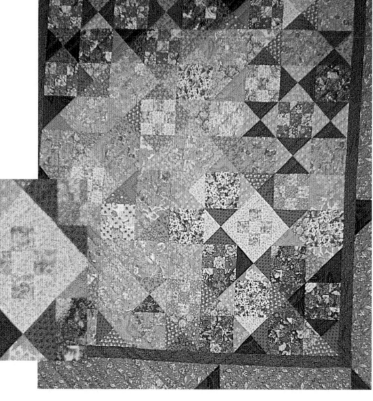

Dianne Newmann

Lessa Siegele

Trudy Billingsley

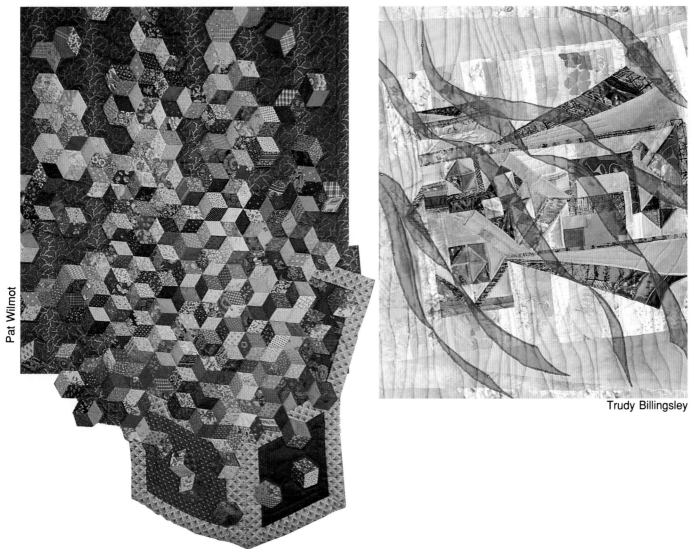

Pat Wilmot

Trudy Billingsley

11

The Quilter's Cupboard

Just like any other craft, successful quilting depends on having the right equipment to do the job. If you are already a sewer, you are more than likely to have some of the things you need at home already – such as a tape measure, needles, scissors and so on. There are, however, a few pieces you will need to buy and it's a good idea to buy the best that you can afford when it comes to equipment you will want to use again and again. There is nothing more frustrating than trying to cut along a straight line with a pair of dull scissors. You'll chew up so much fabric that it would have been cheaper to buy good scissors in the beginning.

This is a list of the equipment you are likely to need, although you may not need everything on the list for every quilt.

SCISSORS

A good pair of scissors is essential and ideally you should have three pairs, including a large pair of dressmaker's shears, a smaller pair for delicate fabrics and the tricky shapes, and a third pair for cutting paper and templates. It is a good idea to reserve your good dressmaker's shears for cutting fabric, to keep them in the best condition.

PINS

Glass-headed pins are ideal for patchwork and quilting. You may like to use pins of different lengths for different purposes. Longer pins are handy for pinning through a number of layers of fabric and batting. Even better than ordinary pins for this purpose, are medium-sized safety pins which hold the work together quite securely and are a speedier solution than basting with a needle and thread. We call this pin-basting.

NEEDLES

For hand-piecing, use a fine needle you are comfortable with. Sharps are suitable for the purpose. For hand-quilting, you will need size 8 or 9 Betweens. As these are quite short there will be times when you may need a longer needle as well and Sharps are again suitable.

For machine-piecing and machine-quilting, you will need a machine needle suitable for the thickness of your fabrics. Be ruthless – throw away needles as soon as they lose their sharpness. In fact, it is a good idea to begin each project with a new needle in any case.

CUTTER

The rotary or Olfa cutter is a great boon to the quilter. A great labor saver, it allows you to cut several layers of fabric at one time without distortion. You should use a rotary cutter in conjunction with a good transparent ruler and a self-healing mat, made especially for the purpose.

RULERS

Avoid wooden rulers and choose one made from plastic or metal instead. The transparent plastic ones have the dual advantages of being quite sturdy and allowing you to see the fabric or paper beneath.

Craft shops sell excellent plastic rulers especially made for quilting that have several marked reference points to assist you to cut straight and accurately. A 3'-4'/1m metal ruler is very helpful for marking long strips and triangles and an L-square will help with drafting.

SEWING MACHINE

Consider your sewing machine as an extension of yourself while stitching a quilt! Your machine needs to be clean and oiled at all times to keep it running properly, and your machine needle needs replacing frequently. Bernina machines with a knee-lift lever for the presser foot are a positive gift to quilters, as they allow you to keep two hands on your work at all times.

THIMBLES

Smooth quilting technique always demands that you use at least one thimble and perhaps two – a metal one for the third finger of the upper hand and a leather one for the finger underneath to protect it.

THREAD

Good quality sewing thread should be used for hand or machine-piecing. For hand-quilting, it is best to use cotton quilting thread. It is stronger than the usual sewing thread and comes in a good variety of colors. In the past, threads have been treated by passing them through beeswax (some books still recommend it) but it is no longer necessary with the excellent quilting threads available today.

The color of the thread for piecing should blend with the fabrics so you can work with only one color and not have to keep re-threading the needle. You can buy nylon monofilament thread at good quilting shops. This has the advantage of being 'invisible' and therefore suitable for all colors. It should only be used as the top thread, with an ordinary sewing thread in the bobbin.

PENCILS

A soft, sharp lead pencil for tracing around templates is essential. These days you can buy water-soluble pencils and pens, especially made for quilters, including a silver pencil that will mark both light and dark fabrics. Make sure that whatever you choose will either fade out or wash out without leaving a permanent mark.

TEMPLATES

A template is a precisely drawn and cut shape for a pattern piece. Some templates for hand-piecing, such as the shell, hexagon and diamond, are available from craft shops but it is not difficult to make your own. If the template is not going to be used too often, then cardboard (perhaps strengthened with tape) is quite suitable. Sandpaper is also useful as it tends to grip the fabric as you work. The problem with both of these options is that they are very subject to wear and tear, especially around the edges. If you do use cardboard, it is a good idea to cut a number of stencils rather than relying on just one. If the template is going to be used many times or if the particular project is a big one, then you would be wise to cut your template out of firm plastic or acetate, available from quilting and art supply shops. Whichever material you choose, you will need the usual drawing aids (set square, protractor, pencil, ruler etc) as well as a sharp craft knife or scissors for cutting out the template. Draw your shape carefully onto the template material, using a ruler to achieve straight lines. Carefully cut out the shape with a sharp craft knife or scissors. In this book, templates for tracing are supplied.

HOOPS AND FRAMES

Quilting hoops are essential on all but the smallest hand-quilted projects to achieve a smooth finish. A quilting hoop consists of two wooden rings, one of which fits closely inside the other. The fabric is stretched over the inner ring and then secured with the outer ring. Take care not to stretch the fabric too tightly. A hoop of about 16"/40 cm is a good size to work with. You can also buy a quilting hoop on a stand or, if the project is a large one, use a free-standing quilting frame if you find one comfortable to work with. You can also buy small hoops, specially made for machine-quilting.

MATERIAL MATTERS

You can always tell a true quilter by the bulging bags and drawers full of fascinating scraps of fabric, squirreled away for future use. And actually, this is one of the most delightful aspects of quilting – that even when you're not actually working on a project, you can be planning and designing, waiting for the coincidence of two scraps of fabric to trigger your imagination.

CHOOSING YOUR FABRIC

A quilt is basically a sandwich with a filling, the batting or wadding, between two layers of fabric. The filling is held in place by the stitches of the quilting or by the tying. Any fabric that keeps its shape when stretched with two hands along the grain, can be used for quilting.

The choice of fabrics and colors is crucial to the success of a quilt. You can use patterns and plains of just about every kind, but some fabrics are obviously better suited than others. Smooth, closely woven, dress-weight cottons are ideal for quilting. Linen, lightweight wool, silk or sateen also work well. Avoid synthetic or stretchy fabrics as they are more difficult to manage. Velvet gives a lovely texture to patchwork, but you will need a little more experience to manage its foibles. Whichever you choose, make sure all your fabrics are of the same, or very similar, weight.

Some quite heavy fabrics, like tweed or wool, can look very effective, but are a great challenge for the hand-quilter. It is best to reserve these for machine-quilting. At the other end of the scale, very sheer fabrics can also give you quilters' nightmares! If you must use one because it is just right and there is no substitute, line it first with a dress-weight cotton.

Small prints, florals and checks, are ideal for quilting, but bolder prints can also be effective. To get an impression of how the finished quilt will look, drape the fabrics over a chair in roughly the proportions you will be using them and then stand back and consider. You will be able to tell how well the colors and patterns work together or whether you need to make changes. Stripes can be very effective, but take care – they will show any faults if your cutting and sewing are not perfectly straight. The difference between a mediocre quilt and an outstanding one often lies in the way the quilter has used light, shade and color to complement the patchwork.

Experiment with combinations of color and pattern – you will learn with experience which combinations work best.

BACKING

Choose an all-cotton fabric for the quilt back, washing and preparing it in the same way as the fabrics for the quilt top. For a large quilt, you may have to join fabrics to achieve the width of backing required. If you are new to quilting, choose a print fabric for the backing rather than a solid one – it is much more forgiving of the odd uneven stitch.

PREPARING YOUR FABRIC

It is crucial to wash (preferably in a washing machine) cotton fabrics before you cut. Washing will pre-shrink the fabric and take out the excess dye and any chemical sizing. The dye in some fabrics can run and stain the others, so wash any likely culprits by hand to test for color fastness. Iron the fabrics while they are still damp. Remove all the selvages before you begin cutting.

BATTING

Batting or wadding as it is also known, is the filling in the 'quilt sandwich'. In days past, any thick material such as flannel or even an old quilt were used for batting. These days the most commonly used batting is made from polyester fiber. It is available in a variety of widths and thicknesses and has the advantage of being lightweight, washable and non-allergenic. Traditional cotton batting is still used but is much heavier than the polyester version and the finished quilt will have to be dry cleaned. Take care with cotton batting because it tends to move around and bunch up in spots. Close quilting will help to prevent this happening. Batting which is not too hard to the touch is the easiest to sew. It should be bonded to prevent fibers migrating through the quilt.

Wool batting gives a wonderful warmth and softness to a quilt. Cotton/polyester batting is also available. Like your quilting fabrics, it has to be pre-washed as the cotton content shrinks. For hand-quilting, it is better to choose the thinner batting, which gives the traditional look, and keep the thicker types for machine-quilted and tied quilts, which sometimes look more like comforters.

15

Quilting Skills

Quilting is not difficult. If you can sew a simple running stitch, you can make a quilt. There are a few simple principles and techniques that will help you.

MARKING FABRIC

Always mark the fabric on the wrong side with a sharp pencil, dark for light fabric and light or silver for dark fabric. Test the marker for washability on a scrap of fabric first. Place the template on the fabric with a straight edge following the grainline. Some templates will even have the grainline marked for you.

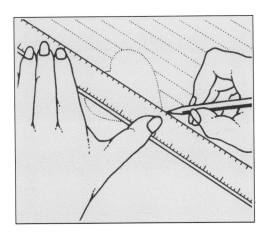

Left: Use a plastic ruler and sharp pencil to mark lines and templates on your fabric

CUTTING OUT

Pieced quilting requires the cutting of dozens of small shapes. The quickest way to cut a quantity of the same piece is to cut three or four thicknesses of fabric together. Using a rotary cutter and cutting mat is the easiest way to cut strips. Otherwise you will need to

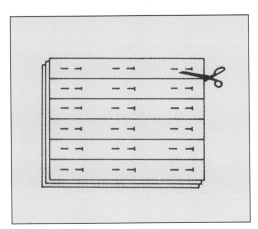

Left: Cutting out a large number of strips using the multi-layered method

pin the fabric layers together, placing the pins inside the cutting line which is marked on the top layer. Cut out the shape carefully with good, sharp scissors,

taking particular care with the corners. This method is only suitable if you can work without marked seamlines. For all hand-piecing and some machine-piecing, penciled seamlines are essential. Trace around the template with a sharp pencil then cut out with a seam allowance added, usually $1/4$"/6 mm. The pencil lines you have drawn become your sewing line.

SEWING

Analyze the quilt pattern so you can piece it in a logical way. (Our directions do this for you.) Assemble the smallest pieces to make larger units, then assemble these to make still larger ones. Plan the assembly to avoid inserting sharply-pointed pieces into tight corners – almost all patterns can be broken into straight lines.

When sewing patchwork, place pieces right sides together. (For appliqué, place all pieces right side up.) If the pieces are square or rectangular sew across the intersecting seam allowances; if they are not, begin and end the stitching right at the intersecting seamlines.

MACHINE-PIECING OR HAND-PIECING

Machine-piecing is the quickest way of joining patchwork but there are occasions when handsewing is preferable, such as when you need to sew in angles or carefully match difficult points. Equally, some quilts are best machine-pieced, such as the *Log Cabin* and *Seminole* designs. In truth, quilters who choose hand-piecing do so, not for practical reasons, but for the pleasure of relaxing hand work and its portability.

Before you begin sewing, you will need to estab-

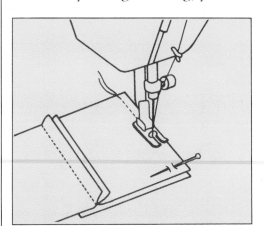

Left: Machine-piecing patches together into a strip

lish a reference for the seam allowance. If the distance from the needle to the edge of the presser foot is $^1/4$"/6 mm, then you can place the edge of the presser foot on the edge of the fabric to achieve the exact seam allowance. If this is not the case on your machine, you can use any lines marked on the foot plate or mark your own with masking tape.

Pin the pieces together with right sides facing, placing the pins at right angles to the seamline. There is no need to backstitch at this stage because seams

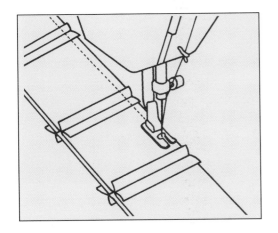

Left: Piecing strips together, sewing across the seams

will be crossed over by others. Sew the patches together along the seamline, sewing right up to the pins. When you have joined patches into a square or strip, you will need to join that square or strip to others and this will involve sewing across seamlines. Pin and sew as before, taking care to match seamlines and points.

To save time, repeat each step as many times as is needed for the whole quilt, feeding the pieces under

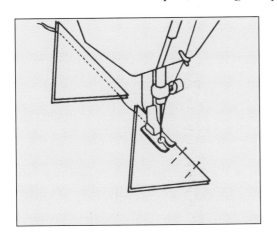

Left: Chainsewing triangles to form pieced squares

the presser foot in a continuous seam. Later, you can cut them apart before joining them in a new combination by the same method – chainsewing.

Hand-piecing is the traditional method of joining patchwork. Pin the patches together with right sides facing, placing the pins at right angles to the seamline.

Sew with small even running stitches, using a size 8 or 9 Sharp needle and quilting or cotton-covered polyester thread. Take care not to have your thread too long – about 16"/40 cm is enough. Begin and end the seam with a few backstitches to secure it. When joining patches, take care to match the pencil lines (seamlines) on both sides, sew only between seamlines and do not stitch in the seam allowances.

PRESSING

Always press seams as you work to keep the pieces flat and the seams as sharp as possible. If you are working with very thick fabric, press the seams open. Generally, however, seams pressed to one side are stronger than those pressed open. Press the seam allowances toward the darker fabric to prevent them showing through the lighter one. Take care not to stretch pieces out of shape when pressing.

CONSTRUCTION

Cut the batting and backing a little larger than the finished size required as the quilting itself draws the fabrics in. You can join lengths of backing fabric to achieve the width you require, after removing all the selvages. Press the seam allowances to one side. The backing can be the same size as the quilt top and then all the edges bound together with a separate binding, or you can have the backing fabric fold onto the quilt front to make a self-binding.

To assemble your quilt, lay the backing fabric face down on a table. Place the batting over the top and then the quilt top on top of that, face up. Smooth out any wrinkles and pin the layers together using medium-sized safety pins or baste for hand-quilting if you prefer.

If you are basting, begin at the center of the quilt and sew towards each corner. Then sew in rows about 4"/10 cm apart over the whole quilt.

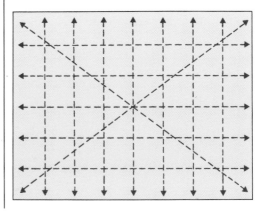

Left: The basting pattern for securing the layers of the quilt

BORDERS

Not all quilts have borders. Some patterns are traditionally made without one, but a border can be used to embellish as well as enlarge a quilt. You can have more than one border. Before you attach the borders, press the quilt top well. Remember the border should look like an integral part of the design, not an afterthought. Choose a fabric that complements the others in the quilt. To work out the length of your side border strips, measure the quilt top lengthwise through the center – not the edges. Cut two borders of the desired width to this length. After attaching these side borders, measure the total width of the quilt top, including the side borders, and cut the top and bottom borders to this length. If you wish to miter the border corners, cut the strips extra long, center them on each end of the quilt, sew them on, then join them with a 45-degree seam at each corner.

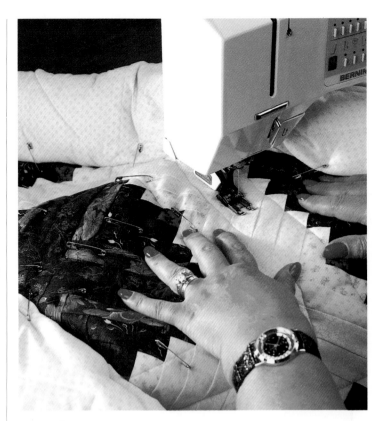

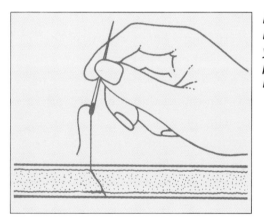

Left: Secure the knotted end of your thread by pulling it into the batting

QUILTING

Quilting by hand should be done using a quilting hoop to keep the layers secure while you work. Use quilting thread color-matched to the fabric unless you want the stitching to show for a special effect. Thread a size 7 or 8 Between sewing needle with about 16"/40 cm of thread and tie a knot in the end. Begin stitching in the center of the quilt, inserting the needle

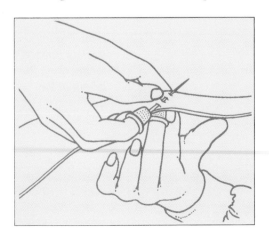

Left: Hand-quilting requires two thimbles for a smooth technique

about ³/4"/2 cm from where you wish to begin. Pull gently on the thread so the knot slips into the batting. Work in small, even running stitches, sewing around the seamlines, outline quilting ¹/4"/1 cm inside the edges of the patches or in patterns that you have drawn onto the fabric. Use a stencil to keep your patterns uniform over the whole of the quilt. When you have finished quilting, end as you began by knotting the thread and running it about ³/4"/2 cm into the batting before cutting it off, even with the fabric. To move from one motif to another, slide the needle under the top layer of your quilt rather than cutting the thread and beginning again.

Machine-quilting is becoming more and more popular. While results appear very quickly, it does have the disadvantage of not being portable. Use a cotton-coated polyester machine sewing thread or a nylon monofilament thread and a size 70 to 90 needle, depending on the thickness of your quilt. You may also need to adjust the stitch length. Do a little test piece to check all your settings. An even-feed walking foot attachment will help to move the layers of your quilt smoothly without effort or bunching. As with hand-quilting, you should begin in the center of your quilt and work toward the edges. To do this, roll the opposite sides up quite tightly on either side of the presser foot leaving the area to be quilted lying flat in the middle. You can then unroll parts as you need them.

BINDING

When all the quilting is complete, trim the batting and backing even with the quilt top (unless you plan to fold the backing over onto the front to make a self binding). Cut your binding strips to the width

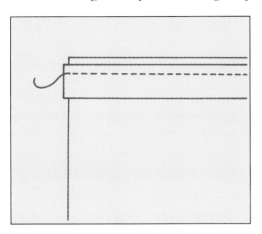

Left: Applying the binding to the top edge of the quilt

suggested and the length required (plus seam allowances) for the top, bottom and sides of the quilt. Fold the strips in half lengthwise, wrong sides together; press. Stitch the binding to the sides of the quilt through all thicknesses, with right sides together and

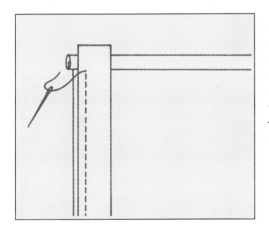

Left: Applying the binding to the side of the quilt, over the top of the previously joined top binding

raw edges even. Fold it to the back of the quilt and slipstitch in place. Repeat for the top and bottom edges, finishing the corners neatly.

MITERING A CORNER

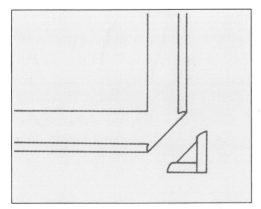

Left: Fold in the raw edge and cut off the corner

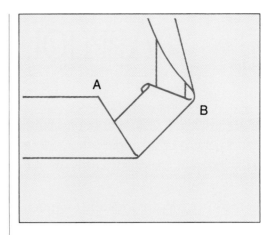

Left: fold in the corner

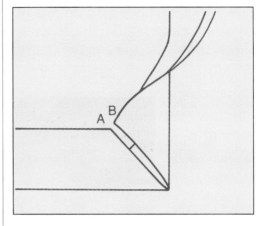

Left: Fold in half the side edges, then fold in the other half so that A meets B

TUFTING OR TYING QUILTS

Some large quilts are not quilted at all in the traditional sense, but are tied. This is particularly useful for quilts where a very thick batting has been used. Using heavy crochet cotton, take a stitch through all the

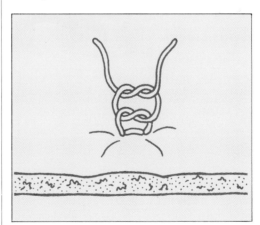

Left: Using thick cotton to tie a quilt

layers of the quilt. Tie the ends together securely twice, but don't pull too tightly. Trim the ends. For very dramatic tufts, use several strands of crochet cotton or pearl cotton. You can tie a quilt using matching or contrasting cotton. Tie in the seamline or in the center of the patch, depending on whether you are making a feature of the tying or not. You can tie your quilt on the top, or on the back if you do not wish the tufts to show.

Appliqué Quilts

Appliqué adds a new dimension to traditional quilting. It can add texture and pattern to a simple whole cloth quilt or embellish a pieced quilt, making it a truly unique object.

Appliqué has been known for centuries and for much of that time it has been part of the quilter's art. The advent of inexpensive printed cotton fabrics gave an almost limitless range to the possibilities. One area in which this development was most obvious was in the flourishing of Broderie Perse quilts. This is a technique in which motifs are cut from printed chintz fabric and arranged to make a new design on a (usually plain) background and appliquéd in place. These quilts often depict the Tree of Life.

The delight of appliqué is that you can use any pattern or design that takes your fancy. There are many traditional designs that are often seen in appliqué quilts, but be adventurous – design your own. A motif from wallpaper, a picture from a book, a design in a shop window are all useful sources. The photocopier and enlarger will be your greatest ally when it comes to designing your appliqué quilt.

HAND-APPLIQUE

When you are cutting pieces for appliqué remember that pieces marked on the wrong side of the fabric will be reversed when turned right-side up. If your pattern piece is not symmetrical, take time to to determine the proper orientation before marking and cutting it out.

To prepare appliqué cut a paper pattern piece (without seam allowance) for each appliqué piece. Trace the outline of the pattern onto the wrong side of the fabric, add seam allowance and cut out. Pin or baste the paper pattern to the wrong side of the piece inside the marked outline. With the tip of your iron, press the seam allowance to the wrong side over the paper, and baste to secure if necessary. (If you wish to make

Broderie Perse, make the paper patterns from tracing paper: Trace the motif from the right side of the fabric and cut it out on the marked line, then cut the motif out carefully, adding seam allowance.)

When all the appliqué pieces are prepared, arrange them on the background fabric. If the pieces overlap to make the design, slipstitch them together at the appropriate points, being careful not to pierce the paper liners. Pin the pieces to the background and slipstitch in place through the fabric only. When you have stitched about three-quarters of the way around each piece, snip the basting, lift the edge of the piece and, using tweezers, pull out the paper patterns; slipstitch the remaining edge of the piece to the background.

Doffy White, who made this wonderful appliqué quilt, made her templates out of pliable plastic so they could easily be removed and re-used without her having to cut hundreds of small paper pieces. She repeated the charming appliqué design in the hand-quilting.

MACHINE-APPLIQUE

Appliqué with a sewing machine is quick and easy. It is crucial to know your sewing machine and all its foibles and to keep it in top working order. Always use sharp needles and keep the machine well oiled. If you have a special walking foot that feeds the fabric evenly through the machine you will find your work even easier. You can also buy a quilting guide for accurate stitching.

If you plan to use a zigzag stitch to appliqué your pieces it is not necessary to add seam allowance to them (or to press under the edges). If you wish, you can bond the pieces to fusible webbing to stabilize them for stitching, but there is no way to remove the webbing and it may add a little bulk. Follow the manufacturer's directions to use fusible webbing.

PREPARING TO QUILT

The stitches that hold the layers of the quilt together add the final touch to any patchwork or appliqué design. The actual quilting pattern can be very important – a part of the overall design – or very simple and unobtrusive – an echo of the piecing. Very often both types are combined on one quilt, with an elaborate pattern filling plain blocks or borders while the patchwork itself is simply outlined. Whatever quilting pattern you choose, it is essential to mark it accurately onto the quilt top before you assemble the quilt's layers.

FINDING THE REPEAT

Before you can mark the quilting design onto the fabric you must check to make sure that it will repeat evenly over the space to be quilted. (The quilting patterns in this book have been planned to repeat evenly as pictured.) If you are quilting a border, measure the width (height) of the quilting pattern to be sure that it fits on the width of the border attractively. Then measure the length of the quilting pattern and divide the length of your border strip by this number. If the result is a whole number, the pattern will repeat evenly; if the division results in a fractional number you will have a partial repeat of the pattern at some point and you may have to adjust it. Be sure you allow for the treatment of the design at the corners before you do too much figuring: Do you want the pattern to miter or butt at the corners, or to stop short so you can fill the corner with another pattern? Be sure to figure the repeat for both the side and the top/bottom dimensions.

If your pattern does not repeat evenly, take the time to figure out best how to alter it. Begin by finding the center of the border and centering the pattern at that point, then repeating it to the end to see where the design breaks. Sometimes a partial repeat at each end of the border strip will look just fine. If not, you may want to take the pattern to a photocopier to enlarge or reduce it slightly, or you may like to add a different quilting pattern at the center or ends of the border to compensate for the uneven repeat. (If your quilting pattern is not a continuous one you can probably just space the motifs a little further apart to adjust the repeat.)

MAKING THE QUILTING MOTIFS

You can make your quilting templates by cutting a shape from acetate or cardboard, but if the pattern you have chosen is at all complex you may find it easier to work with a stencil. If you make your stencil from acetate you will be able to see through it, which is very helpful when positioning the design on the quilt.

Choose a piece of acetate which is a little larger in each dimension than the quilting pattern and mark the outline of the space to be quilted on it. (In other words, mark the width of the border and the length of the repeat, or the dimensions of a plain square.) This will help you to position the stencil on the quilt. Then center and trace the pattern inside the outline. Place the acetate on a cutting mat and cut a narrow groove along each line, just wide enough to pass your pencil through, being sure to leave some connecting bridges from time to time so the stencil doesn't fall apart.

MARKING THE FABRIC

Press your quilt top and place it face up on a table. Place the stencil over the appropriate areas and mark through it with the marker of your choice. Since the quilting will probably take you a while, it is probably best not to use the kind of marker that evaporates in 48 hours, but do be sure that whatever you use can be removed once the quilting is complete. It is a good idea to work from the center of each border towards the ends. Be sure to mark the entire quilt top before assembling the layers.

A NOTE ON THE MEASUREMENTS IN THIS TEXT

For the convenience of all readers, the measurements and dimensions in the following instructions are given in both inches and metrics. The two sets of measurements have been figured to the closest equivalents and adjusted so that the pieces will fit together properly using either system. However, please remember that the two sets of figures are not interchangeable; choose one type as a guide and use it to complete an entire quilt, don't switch in the middle. Along the same lines, there may be some slight variation in the overall finished size from one system to the other.

Traditional Quilts

For centuries, piecing fabrics together into quilts of intricate design has been a much-loved craft. Few examples of the earliest patchwork quilts remain, but the more recent history is richly illustrated with beautiful pieces such as these.

LOG CABIN QUILTS

Log Cabin quilts are among the most popular traditional quilt patterns. Follow Kate McEwen's step-by-step guide to making your own Log Cabin quilt on the following pages.

Log Cabin quilts are ideal for beginners and the pattern can be easily adapted to smaller projects such as cushions, pot holders and placemats. Our step-by-step quilt is a *Log Cabin* quilt in the *Barn Raising* style, one of the most popular quilt patterns. It can be a true scrapbag quilt, utilizing quite small pieces of fabric where the only governing factor is the contrast between light and dark colors.

Like all *Log Cabin* quilts, it is based on the pattern of light and dark rectangles, pieced around a center square. The rectangles are laid in such a way as to represent the logs used by the early American settlers to build their cabins. Some early quilts even

had a little chimney sewn in to further underline the theme. The center square of the block is often red, to denote the fireplace, or yellow, to represent the lighted window.

These days, most *Log Cabin* quilts are made from light and dark printed, dress-weight cottons but, in the past, quilters often used wool as well. Mixing silks, velvets, and other 'luxury' fabrics produces a lovely quilt with quite a different feeling about it. Traditional *Log Cabin* quilts were made without a border, but this is not a hard-and-fast rule and these days quilters often add a solid or print border.

While the basic *Log Cabin* block is always divided diagonally into four quarters – two of dark and two of light rectangles – changing the way in which the colors are placed or the blocks are joined will give you quite a different looking quilt. Usually the blocks are placed so the two light quarters are adjacent and diagonally opposite the two dark quarters. Joining these blocks so that four dark halves are adjacent to one another and four light halves are adjacent to one another gives a design of alternating light and dark diamonds. Joining them so that the dark and light halves form alternating concentric diagonals makes this design known as *Barn Raising*. Placing the blocks so that the dark and light halves alternate diagonally all the way across the quilt creates the pattern known as *Straight Furrows*.

Left: Make this Log Cabin quilt following the instructions on pages 26-29

Left: A charming Log Cabin quilt combining subtle colors and prints for a real country look

Below left: This charming placemat is simply one Log Cabin block with a stenciled design painted into the center square. To complete the placemat, assemble the top, batting, backing and binding as for a quilt

Below: Log Cabin quilts depend on the arrangement of light and dark fabrics for their effect

CREATE A QUILT

FINISHED SIZE
Quilt: 71" x 90"/180 cm x 225 cm
Block size: 9"/22.5 cm square
Total number of full blocks: 48

FABRIC QUANTITIES
$^1/_4$ yd/20 cm of color 1 (red)
$^1/_4$ yd/20 cm of color 2 (dark)
$^1/_3$ yd/30 cm of color 3 (light)
$^1/_2$ yd/40 cm of color 4 (dark)
$^1/_2$ yd/45 cm of color 5 (light)
$^2/_3$ yd/55 cm of color 6 (dark)
$1^2/_3$ yds/1.5 m of color 7 (light), this
    includes fabric for the first border
$1^1/_3$ yds/1.2 m of color 8 (dark), this
    includes fabric for the second
    border
74" x 92"/185 cm x 230 cm backing
    fabric, pieced from $5^1/_4$ yds/4.6 m
    of 45"/115 cm wide fabric
74" x 92"/185 cm x 230 cm batting
an additional $^2/_3$ yd/60 cm of color 8
    for the binding

NOTIONS
safety pins, pins, needles and scissors
sewing thread
sewing machine
pencil and ruler
rotary (Olfa) cutter and mat

CUTTING
$^1/_4$"/6 mm seam allowances are included in the cutting instructions.

1 Cut your fabric into strips by folding the fabric in half, selvage to
selvage, and then again so you have
four layers. If you are using a rotary
(Olfa) cutter you can put about three
lots of fabric, folded this way, on top
of each other and cut them all at once.
An Olfa cutter is ideal for a *Log Cabin*
quilt and means that seam allowances
are already included in the cutting
instructions. Cut all the fabric into
$1^5/_8$"/4 cm wide strips. You will need:
2 strips of red, cut into $1^1/_2$"/4 cm
    squares
5 strips of color 2
7 strips of color 3
9 strips of color 4
11 strips of color 5
13 strips of color 6
16 strips of color 7
19 strips of color 8

Step 2

CONSTRUCTION

2 Take the pile of red squares and
one strip of colour 2. Lay the strip
under the presser foot of your sewing

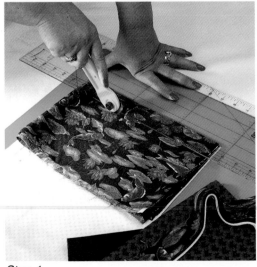

Step 1

*Step 1: Using a specially
marked plastic ruler, rotary
cutter and mat to cut multiple
fabric layers*
*Step 2: Chainsewing all the
red squares to the first dark
strip*

machine (right side up) and lay the red squares on top one by one (right side down), stitching them together in a $^1/4"$/ 6 mm seam. Sew all the red squares in this way. Press the seams and cut the strip between (and even with the edges of) the red squares, so each red square is joined to a color-2 square.

Step 3

3 Take the other strips of color 2 and lay them down one by one (face up) under your presser foot and sew the previously joined red and color 2 squares down onto these strips. Always place the segment just sewn at the top, when placing the block on the next strip to be sewn. Finger press the seams to lie flat. Cut the strip between (and even with the edges of) the dark- and red- squares.

Step 4

Step 3: Joining the piece made in Step 2 to another dark strip
Step 4: Using exactly the same procedure as in Step 3, join in the first light strip
Step 5: The completed block for the quilt, with the red square slightly off center. Note that there are two more dark strips than there are light strips in the block

4 Place the first light strip (color 3) under the presser foot as you did for the color 2 strip and join the just completed squares as before. Cut them apart, even with the edges as before. Finger press the seams to lie flat.

5 Add the second strip of color 3 as before and continue in this way, sewing two strips of the same color to each square until all the colors have been sewn to the block. Always place at the top the segment just sewn, when placing the block on the next strip to be sewn. Finger press the seams to lie flat. Cut the strip between (and even with the edges of) those made in the previous step.

Step 5

6 When the forty-eight blocks are complete, arrange them, six blocks across and eight blocks down, as shown for the *Barn Raising* pattern. Sew the blocks together, making sure to match the seams where necessary. Press the quilt top carefully.

7 Attach a border to your quilt if you feel it needs one. Borders can be used to extend a quilt to whatever size you need. We have used two borders – one out of light fabric $3^1/2"$/ 8.8 cm wide and the other out of dark fabric $5^1/2"$/13.8 cm wide. To make the light border, measure the length of

your quilt top through the center. Cut two strips of fabric this length and 4"/10 cm wide. Join fabric if necessary to make the required length. Sew these to the side edges of the quilt top with $1/4$"/6 mm seams. Measure the total width of the quilt top, including the borders you have just joined on, again measuring through the center. Cut two 4"/10 cm wide strips of fabric this length, joining strips if necessary. Sew these to the top and bottom edges of the quilt with $1/4$"/6 mm seams. Make the dark border in exactly the same way, cutting the strips 6"/15 cm wide.

QUILTING

8 Place backing fabric on a table, right side down and secure it with tape. Place the batting on top and then the pieced quilt on top of that, right side up. Pin through all three layers with safety pins to hold the quilt together while you are machine or hand-quilting. *Log Cabin* quilts can also be tied in the traditional way. We have quilted this quilt by machine, stitching diagonally through the center of each block, changing the direction of the diagonal for each quarter of the quilt. Extend the stitching through the light border as well. Make another row of stitches in between each pair of rows just made. The dark border has

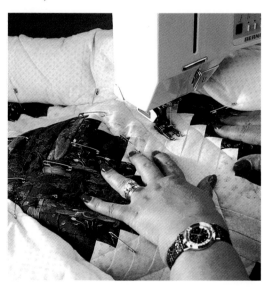

Step 8

been quilted with rows of parallel stitching about 2"/5 cm apart. Trim away any excess batting and backing.

FINISHING

9 To bind the edges of the quilt, cut four $3^1/4$"/8 cm wide strips for the top, bottom and sides. Measure through the center of the quilt as before to determine the length of the strips. Join strips if necessary to achieve the required length. Press the strips in half lengthwise, wrong sides together. Sew the binding to the right side of both sides of the quilt with raw edges even. Fold it over to the wrong side and slipstitch in place. Sew the binding to the top and bottom edges in the same way, finishing the corners neatly.

Above: Detail of the diagonal machine-quilting
Step 8: Quilting by machine, showing the quilted parts rolled up out of the way

SINGLE IRISH CHAIN

Margot Child designed and made this beautiful quilt which is simplicity itself. Made from only two fabrics, a creamy white and contrasting crisp blue cotton, it relies for its charm on the delicate stitching of the hand-quilting.

FABRIC SUGGESTIONS

The blocks in this quilt are set at an angle, traveling diagonally across the quilt. For a slightly different look, make this quilt in two tones of the same color.

The quilt has been machine-pieced and hand-quilted.

FINISHED SIZE

Quilt: 85" x 76"/215 cm x 190 cm
Block size: 6"/15 cm square
Total number of blocks: 162
Total number of border triangles: 34
Total number of half triangles: 4

FABRIC QUANTITIES

4¹/₂ yds/4 m of 45"/115 cm wide
    white fabric
2¹/₄ yds/2 m of 45"/115 cm wide blue
    fabric
89" x 80"/225 cm x 200 cm backing
    fabric, pieced from 4¹/₂ yds/4 m of
    45"/115 cm wide fabric
89" x 78"/225 cm x 200 cm batting

NOTIONS

cardboard or template plastic
pencil and ruler
rotary (Olfa) cutter and mat
safety pins, pins, needles and scissors
sewing thread and quilting thread
sewing machine

CUTTING

Do not forget to add ³/₈"/1 cm seam allowances to each piece you cut.

1 Cut ninety white fabric squares 6"/15 cm plus seam allowances. Cut thirty-eight blue fabric triangles from template **a**, adding seam allowances on all sides. Cut four blue fabric half-triangles from template **b** for the corners adding seam allowances on all sides. Cut strips of blue and white fabric 2"/5cm wide plus seam allowances.

With this quilt it is particularly important to match the grainlines on the template and fabric in order not to be left with a bias edge on your quilt.

CONSTRUCTION

2 Piece the strips together in threes, one-third with two whites and a blue in the middle and two-thirds with two blues and a white in the middle. Press the seams to the blue side. Cut the joined strips into 2"/5 cm lengths plus seam allowances.

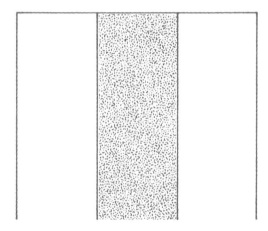

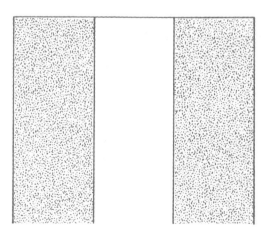

3 Join the strips made in Step 2 in a checkerboard pattern to make seventy-two 9-patch blocks, each with a blue square in the center. Press.

4 Join these blocks to form rows, alternating large white squares with the checkerboard blocks and placing a white square on each end. Press. Note that the number of blocks in a row depends on the position of the row in the quilt. You will need: two single white blocks; two rows of three blocks; two rows of five blocks; two rows of seven blocks; two rows of nine blocks; two rows of eleven blocks; two rows of thirteen blocks, two rows of fifteen blocks and two rows of seventeen blocks.

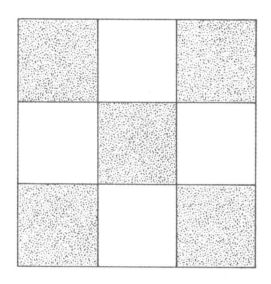

5 At this point it is a good idea to lay your quilt out as it will look when finished. Pin the short side of a blue triangle to the end of each row, so that the long sides of all the triangles form the straight sides of the quilt. Sew the triangles in place. Press.

6 Join all the rows to form the quilt top, sewing a blue half-triangle to every corner square. Press the quilt top carefully.

QUILTING

7 One quilting design appears on the opposite page, two others are on page 34. Trace the quilting designs and make stencils/templates of them, using firm plastic. Transfer the designs to the quilt top using the template and a lead pencil.

8 Lay the backing fabric face down on a table. Place the batting on top and then the quilt top, face up, on top of that. Baste or pin-baste all the layers together.

9 Hand-quilt the quilt top, stitching along the pencil lines and approximately $1/4"/6$ mm inside the small squares as shown.

FINISHING

10 Trim the quilt top and batting so that approximately $1^1/4"/$ 3 cm of the backing fabric protrudes all around. Fold the backing over onto the quilt top, folding in the corners twice to form a neat miter (see page 19). Turn under $1/2"/1$ cm on the raw edge and slipstitch the folded edges and the corners into place.

Left: Detail of the Single Irish Chain quilt showing the hand-quilting

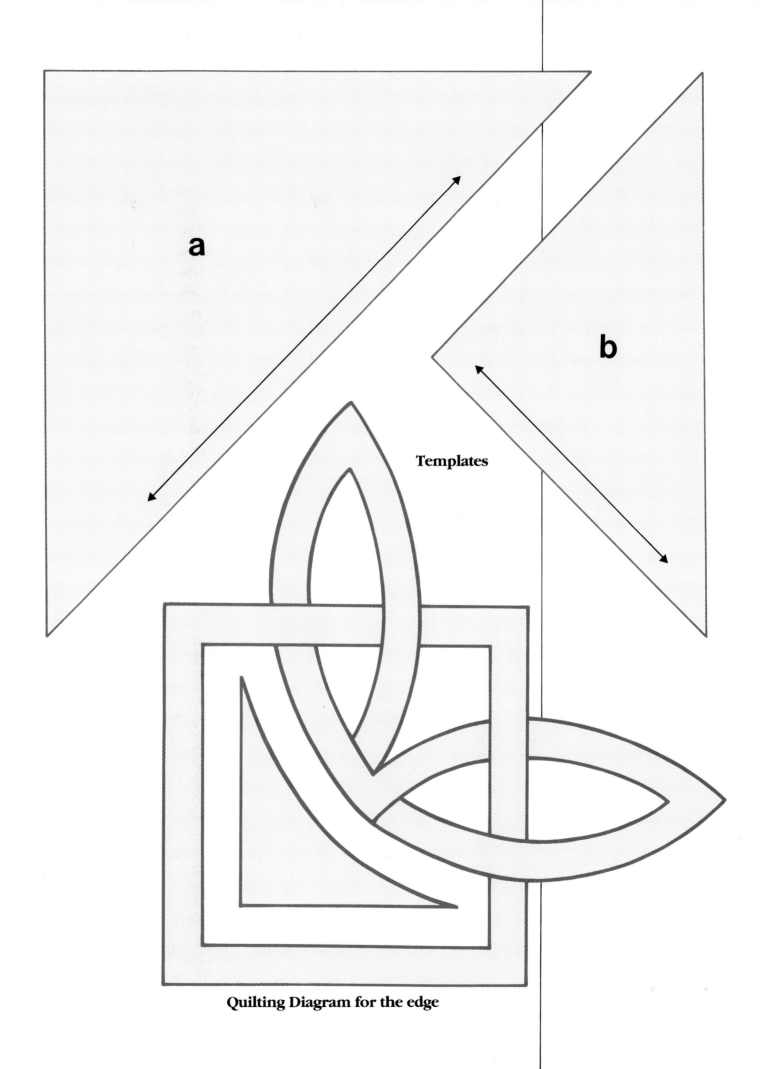

a

b

Templates

Quilting Diagram for the edge

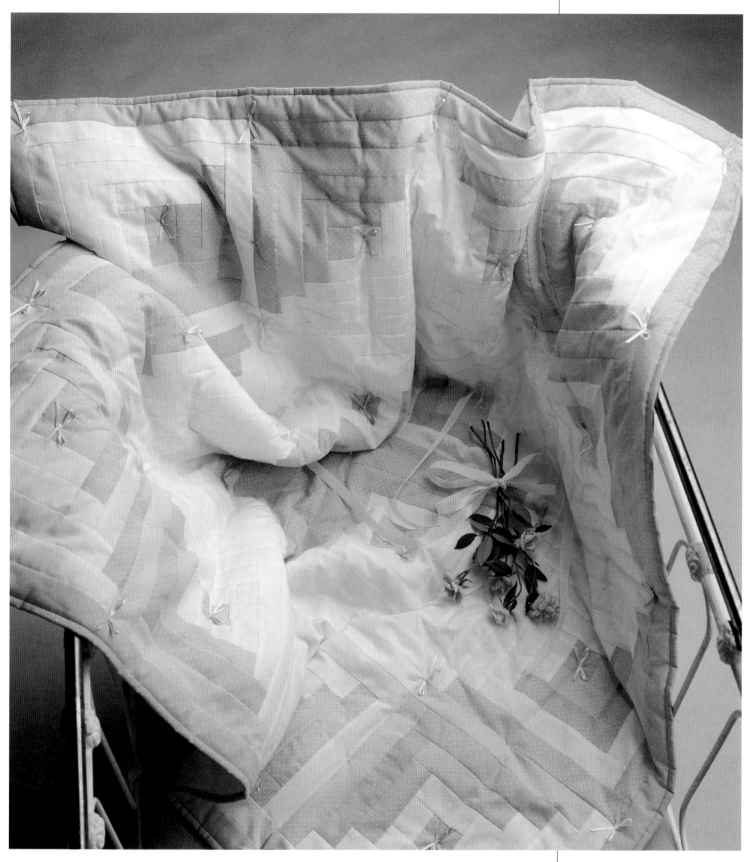

This log cabin quilt has been made using the same spotted voile in five different colors, combined with white. To finish, the quilt has been tied with tiny satin bows in complementary colors

TIED PATCHES

Marie Grove designed and made this quilt by piecing rectangles of brightly colored cotton and then hand-tying them in the traditional way. You can make this bright and cheerful quilt in a weekend. Quilt it by sewing in the ditches of the seams between the patches or hand-quilting a design over the whole quilt top.

FINISHED SIZE
Quilt: 56" x 81"/140 cm x 200 cm
Block size: 8" x 12"/20 cm x 30 cm

FABRIC QUANTITIES
scraps of cotton fabric, in as many
    colors as possible
60" x 85"/150 cm x 210 cm backing
    fabric, pieced from $3^1/3$ yds/3 m of
    45"/115 cm wide fabric
$1^2/3$ yds/1.5 m black fabric for the
    borders and binding
60" x 85"/150 cm x 210 cm batting

NOTIONS
thick crochet cotton for tying
safety pins, pins, needles and scissors
rotary (Olfa) cutter and mat
plastic ruler and pencil
sewing thread
sewing machine

CUTTING
Do not forget to add seam allowances to each piece you cut.

1 Cut the scraps into 36 rectangles to 8" x 12"/20 cm x 30 cm plus seam allowances.

CONSTRUCTION
2 Lay out your quilt top (with six rectangles across and six down) and experiment with the arrangement. Join the top row together and then the next row. Continue in this way until you have six rows. Press. Mark them 1, 2, 3, 4, 5 and 6.

3 Join the six rows to complete the quilt top, following the order you have marked. Press.

4 Measure the width of the quilt top, measuring through the center. Cut two strips of black fabric, each $3^1/2$"/9 cm plus seam allowances wide and as long as this measurement. Sew these to the top and bottom of the quilt top. Measure the length through the center, including the top and bottom borders. Cut two strips of black fabric $3^1/2$"/9 cm wide plus seam allowances and as long as this measurement. Sew these to the sides of the quilt. Press the quilt top.

5 Lay the backing fabric on a table, face down, and place the batting on top. Place the quilt top on top of that, face upwards. Baste or pin-baste through all thicknesses.

TYING
6 Using heavy crochet cotton, take a stitch at each corner of the rectangles. Tie the ends together twice securely, but don't pull too tightly. Trim the ends. For a more dramatic effect, use several strands of thread. Tie again at the center of each rectangle. Trim off any excess backing and batting even with the top.

FINISHING
7 Measure the width of the quilt as before, to find the length of binding required. Cut two strips of black fabric, each $3^1/4$"/8 cm wide and as long as this measurement. Press the strips in half lengthwise, wrong sides together. Sew the binding to the top and bottom of the quilt with right sides facing and raw edges even. Fold the binding to the wrong side and slipstitch into place. Repeat this process for binding the side edges.

Bits and Pieces

This delightfully 'homey' quilt was made from an almost countless variety of cotton seersucker prints which were popular for pyjamas in the 1950s and 1960s. Dorothy Mitchell was lucky enough to acquire them, brand new, in the form of a sample book which had somehow been put away and forgotten.

FABRIC SUGGESTIONS
The same design would lend itself just as well to any small prints, gingham or checks but not to a large print fabric. It is an ideal project for strip cutting, using a rotary cutter. $1/4$"/6 mm seam allowances have been included.

FINISHED SIZE
Quilt: 69" x 84"/175 cm x 213 cm
Block size: $13^{1}/2$"/34 cm square
Total number of full blocks: 12

FABRIC QUANTITIES
a wide variety of cotton print fabrics
$2^{1}/4$ yds/2 m of printed cotton fabric for the borders
72" x 87"/185 cm x 225 cm cotton fabric for the backing (pieced from 4 yds/3.7 m of 45"/115 cm wide fabric)
72" x 87"/185 cm x 225 cm batting

NOTIONS
rotary (Olfa) cutter and mat
plastic ruler
safety pins, pins, needles and scissors
sewing thread
sewing machine

CUTTING
1 Cut 2"/5 cm wide strips across the width of the cotton print fabrics.

CONSTRUCTION
2 Join three 2"/5 cm wide strips together to form a strip 5"/2.5 cm wide. Press.

3 Cut this strip along its length into 5"/12.5 cm squares.

4 Repeat steps 1 and 2, varying the fabric combinations, until you have 108 squares.

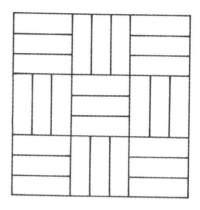

5 To form the block, join nine of these squares into rows of three, alternating horizontal and vertical strips, making a block 14"/35.4 cm square.

6 Join several 2"/5 cm wide strips at their short ends to form a long strip. From this long strip, cut 8 sashes each 14"/35.4 cm long. Do not worry too much about where the seams fall – it is interesting to have them fall in an irregular way.

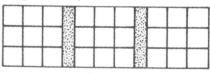

Step 7

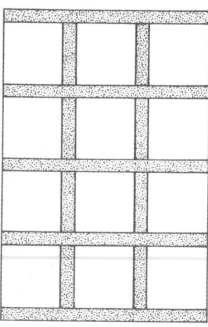

Step 8

38

39

7 Join three blocks horizontally with sashing strips between each pair. Make three more rows the same way.

8 Measure across the center of these rows to determine the length and cut five sashing strips (from the 2"/5 cm wide strip) to this length. Join the four rows of blocks together, placing lengths of sashing strips between them and along the top and the bottom as well. Press.

9 Measure the length of the quilt top through the center. Cut two sashing strips (from the 2"/5 cm wide strip) to this length. Sew one to each side of the quilt top. Press.

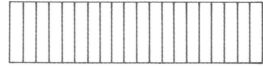

4³/₄"/12 cm

10 Measure the width of the quilt top through the center as before to determine the length of the pieced top and bottom border. Make two panels of pieced strips 4³/₄"/12 cm wide and this length. Stitch a panel across the top and bottom of the quilt. Press.

11 Measure the length of the quilt top through the center, including the sewn-on panels, to determine the length of the pieced side borders. Make two panels of pieced strips 4³/₄"/12 cm wide and this length. Sew one to each side of the quilt top, sewing across the edges of the pieces recently joined to the top and bottom. Press.

12 Measuring through the center as before, cut lengths of the 2"/5 cm wide stripping and sew them to the top and bottom of the quilt. Repeat for both sides. Press.

13 Measure the width of the quilt top through the center and cut two pieces of border fabric to this length and 6"/15 cm wide. Sew them to the top and bottom of the quilt top. Repeat the procedure for the side borders. Press the quilt top carefully.

QUILTING

14 Make a template of the triangle quilting pattern opposite. Mark these triangles as shown around the border.

15 Pin-baste the batting to the wrong side of the quilt top. Place the backing fabric onto the right side of the quilt top and sew around the edges, leaving a small opening for turning. Trim the corners. Turn the quilt right side out. Close the opening by hand. Press.

16 Pin-baste at regular intervals all over the quilt. Machine-quilt around each small square and all printed borders. Hand-quilt along the marked triangles in the plain border.

17 From the remaining length of stripping, cut twenty 2"/5 cm squares. Press in the seam allowances on the raw edges and slipstitch over the junctions of the inner sashing as shown.

TIP

The method given here is one way to complete a quilt. Another way, which you may find easier, is to assemble the three layers of the quilt and then bind the edges with a narrow strip of fabric as described in the *Single Irish Chain* quilt on page 30.

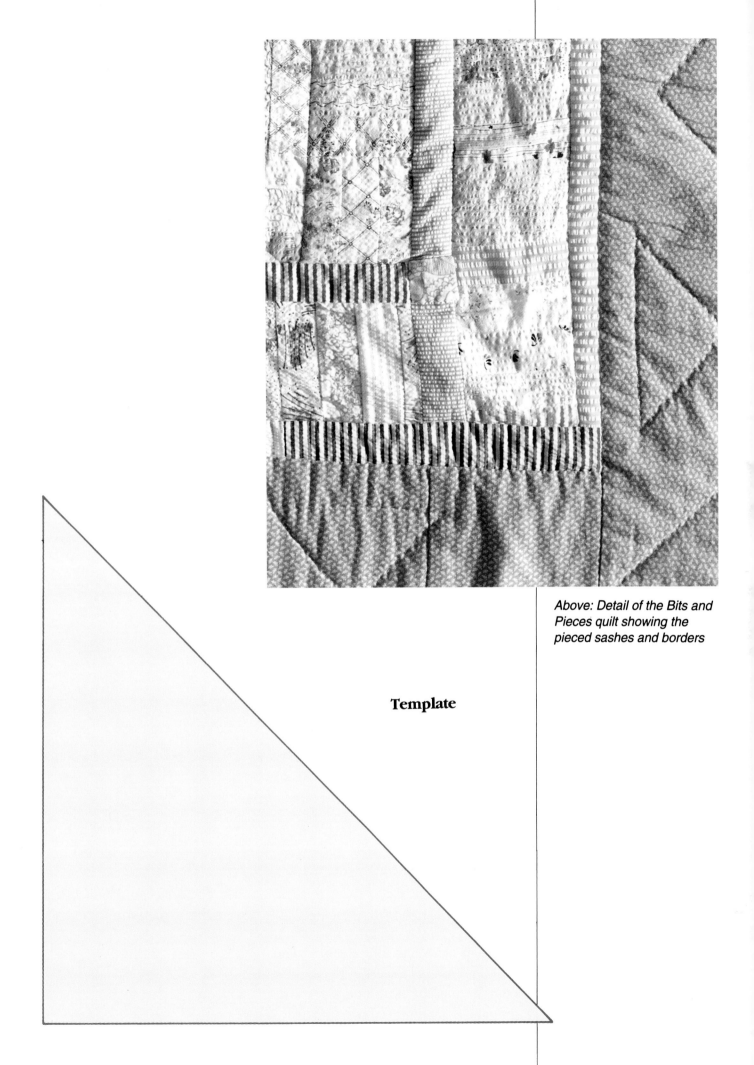

Above: Detail of the Bits and Pieces quilt showing the pieced sashes and borders

Template

OHIO STARS

Graceful hand-quilting is perfect for a simple pattern like the one in this quilt, designed and made by Dorothy Ison.

FABRIC SUGGESTIONS

Choose a dark and a medium print to define the stars on a plain cream background; a third print for the border and a solid fabric for the binding.

FINISHED SIZE

Quilt: 48" x 60"/120 cm x 150 cm
Block size: 12"/30 cm square
Total number of blocks: 12

FABRIC QUANTITIES

$1^2/3$ yds/1.5 m of 45"/115 cm wide cream fabric
$^2/3$ yd/50 cm of 45"/115 cm wide dark print fabric
$^2/3$ yd/50 cm of 45"/115 cm wide medium print fabric
1 yd/80 cm of 45"/115 cm wide print fabric for the borders
$^2/3$ yd/60 cm of 45"/115 cm wide solid fabric for binding
$2^3/4$ yds/2.5 m of 45"/115 cm wide fabric for backing, pieced to be 50" x 62"/125 cm x 155 cm
50" x 62"/125 cm x 155 cm batting

NOTIONS

cardboard or template plastic
pencil and ruler
safety pins, pins, needles and scissors
sewing thread and quilting thread
sewing machine

CUTTING

Do not forget to add seam allowances to each piece you cut.

1 Using the cardboard or plastic trace and cut out the templates. For each block, cut four cream squares and one print square from template **a**; eight print triangles and eight cream triangles from template **b**. You will have six squares each in the two star prints, forty-eight cream squares, forty-eight triangles in each star print and ninety-six triangles in cream.

CONSTRUCTION

2 Chainsew the plain and print triangles together in pairs along one short side. Cut them apart. Press the seams to one side.

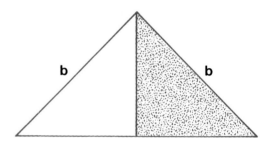

3 Join similar pairs along the long side to form a square, matching points and seams. Press.

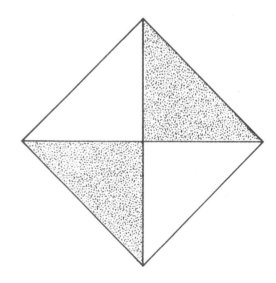

4 Taking the square just made, sew a cream square onto each colored side. Press. Make two such strips, using the same print for each block.

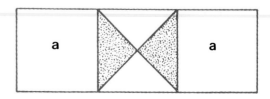

43

5 Sew two of the squares made in Step 3 to opposite sides of a matching print square. Press.

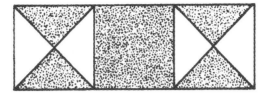

6 Join the pieces made in Steps 4 and 5 to make the complete block. Press. Make six blocks in each star print.

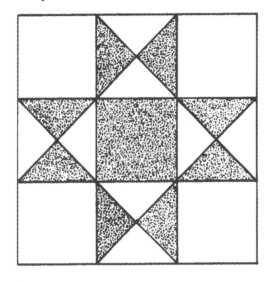

7 Join the blocks in rows of three blocks across, alternating the prints, to make the quilt top.

8 Measure the width of the quilt, measuring through the center. Cut two 4"/10 cm wide strips of the border fabric to this length plus seam allowances. Sew these borders to the top and bottom of the quilt top. Measure the length of the quilt top, measuring through the center and including the top and bottom borders. Cut two 4"/10 cm wide strips of the border fabric to this length plus seam allowances. Sew these to the sides of the quilt top. Press.

QUILTING

9 Using cardboard or template plastic, trace and cut out templates from the quilting patterns on page 46.

Using the templates, mark the design onto the center of each cream square and along the borders.

10 Lay the backing fabric, face down, on a table. Place the batting on top and the quilt top on top of that, face up. Baste or pin-baste all the layers together.

11 Quilt the marked designs on the cream squares and the borders. Hand-quilt along the seamlines and diagonally through the cream squares as shown.

12 Trim off any excess backing and batting.

FINISHING

13 Measure the quilt through the center as before and cut binding fabric 4"/10 cm wide plus seam allowances and the length of these measurements. Press the binding strips in half, wrong sides together. Place binding along the top and bottom edges of the quilt with right sides together and raw edges even. Stitch the bindings in place. Repeat for the side bindings, finishing the corners neatly.

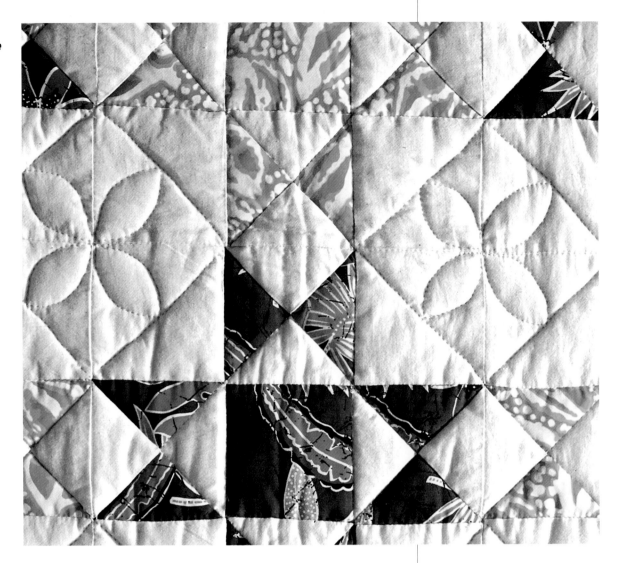

Right: Detail of the Stars quilt showing the hand-quilting

Templates

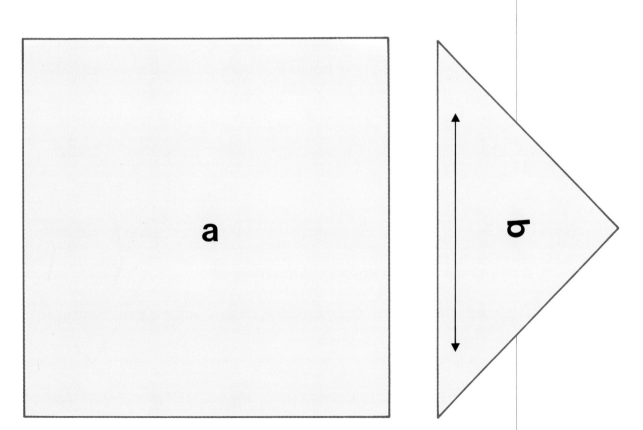

a

q

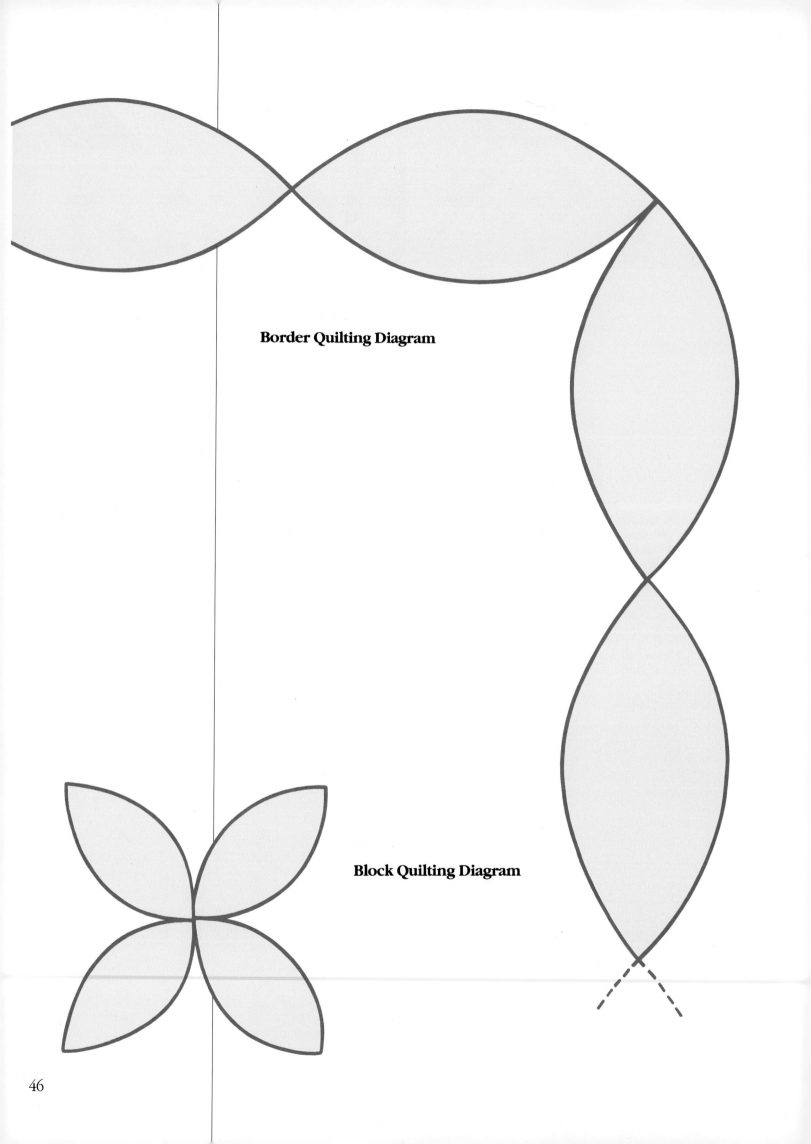

Border Quilting Diagram

Block Quilting Diagram

This very simple quilt has been made using fabrics with a Japanese feel. The bolster pillow has been appliquéd and embroidered to match

BASKET QUILT

Vicki Cordony is the proud owner of this fine example of a wonderful quilting tradition – the friendship quilt. Eight people contributed blocks to this hand-pieced and hand-quilted quilt.

FABRIC SUGGESTIONS

Use various colored, cotton fabrics, with checks and stripes on a cream background. The blocks are set on the diagonal. For the background and backing, choose a homespun cloth.

FINISHED SIZE

Quilt: 60" x 70"/150 cm x 176 cm
Block size: 7"/18 cm square
Total number of full blocks: 72
Total number of corner blocks: 4
Total number of border blocks: 22 half blocks

FABRIC QUANTITIES

$2^7/8$ yds/2.5 m of 45"/115 cm wide cotton background fabric
$1^2/3$ yds/1.5 m of various 45"/115 cm wide printed fabrics for the baskets
64" x 74"/160 cm x 185 cm batting
$3^3/4$ yds/3.2 m of cotton fabric (pieced to make 64" x 74"/160 cm x 185 cm) for the backing
$1/2$ yd/.5 m of 45"/115 cm wide cotton fabric for binding

NOTIONS

cardboard or template plastic
pencil and ruler
safety pins, pins, needles and scissors
sewing thread and quilting thread
sewing machine

CUTTING

Do not forget to add seam allowance to each piece you cut.

1 Cut templates **a**, **b**, **c**, **d**, and **e** from cardboard or template plastic. Lay the templates on the back of the fabric, matching grainlines on the fabric and templates. Draw around the templates with a sharp pencil. This pencil line will be the sewing line. Cut out with a $1/4$"/6 mm seam allowance.

2 *For each block*: Cut
template **a**	1 print	
	1 plain background	
template **b**	2 print	
	2 plain background	
template **c**	3 plain background	

For the corner blocks: Cut
template **d**	4 plain background	

For the half blocks: Cut
template **e**	22 plain background	

For each handle, cut a bias strip 7"/18 cm long and $1^1/4$"/3 cm wide from print fabric. Press under $1/4$"/3 cm on the raw edges on each side.

CONSTRUCTION

3 Appliqué a handle to one plain piece **a** along the dotted line with slipstitch. Sew the inner curve first. Trim the ends. Press.

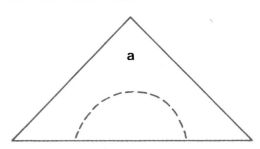

4 Join the handle triangle to the print triangle of the same size to form the handle square. Press.

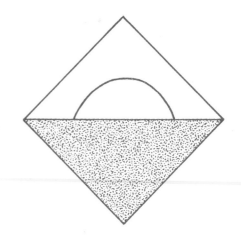

5 *To make Strip 1*: Join a print triangle **b** to a plain triangle **b** to make a square. Sew a plain square **c** to each side of the pieced square as shown. Press.

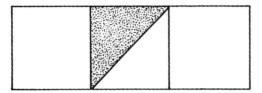

6 *To make Strip 2*: Join a print triangle **b** to a plain triangle **b** to make a square. Sew a plain square **c** to this square as shown. Press.

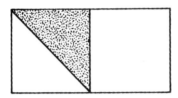

7 *To assemble the block*: Lay the handle square with the handle uppermost. Join Strip 2 to the lower right side of the handle square and

Strip 1 to the lower left side, sewing across the end of Strip 2. Press.

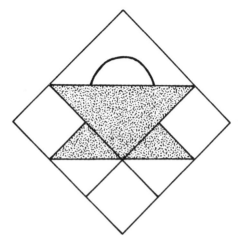

8 Lay out the 72 blocks in a pleasing color arrangement. Join them together, adding in the corner blocks and half blocks. Press.

QUILTING

9 Lay the backing fabric face down on a table, with the batting on top. Place the pieced quilt top on top of that, face up. Smooth out any wrinkles. Baste or pin-baste through all the layers.

10 Hand-quilt the printed fabric into 1"/2.5 cm squares, and the background along the seamlines.

11 Trim off any excess backing and batting.

FINISHING

12 *For the binding*: Cut the fabric into 3"/7 cm wide strips. Join strips together to achieve the desired lengths to bind the sides first and then the top and bottom, measuring through the center of the quilt lengthways and widthways to determine the lengths required. Fold the strips in half, wrong sides together and raw edges even. Press. Sew the binding to the front of the quilt, with raw edges matching, and fold the pressed edge to the wrong side. Slipstitch the pressed edge to the back of the quilt.

Below: A detail of the Basket Quilt showing the diagonal quilting

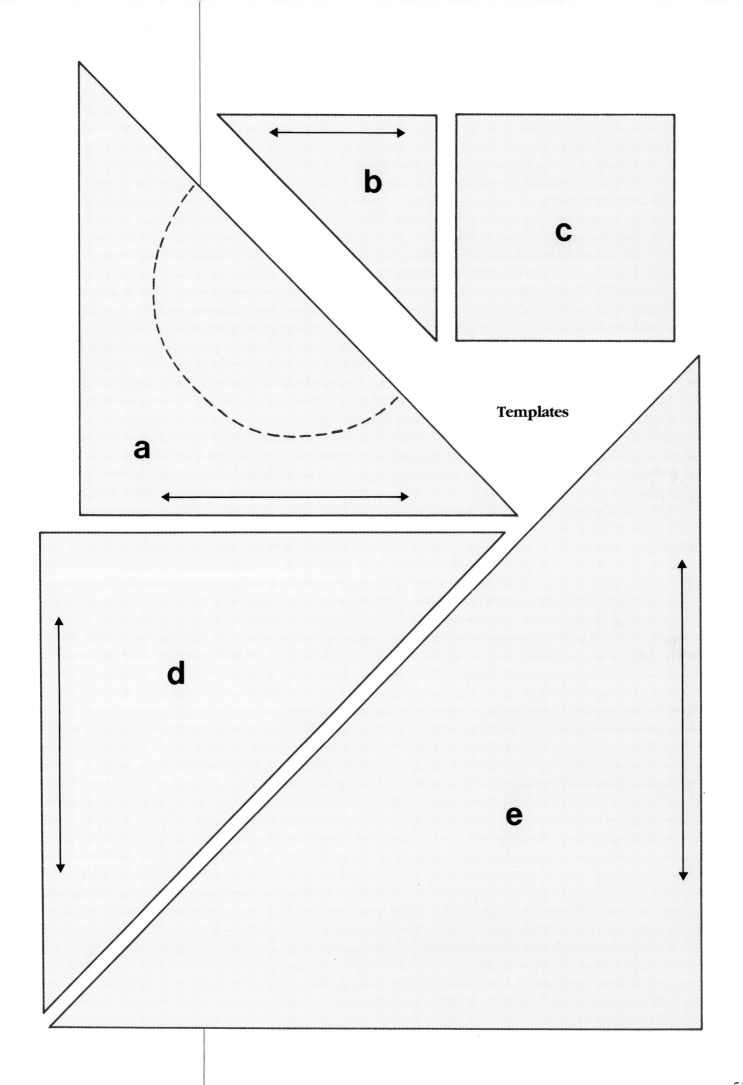

b

c

Templates

a

d

e

SQUARE-IN-SQUARE

Beryl Hodges used a multitude of 'country' fabrics in stripes and checks in muted blues, greens, reds and browns for this charming quilt, which has been machine-pieced and machine-quilted.

FABRIC SUGGESTIONS

The fabric is dress-weight cotton in light, medium and dark tones. See how some of the fabrics have been used slightly off-grain for added interest and to keep the eye moving around the quilt.

FINISHED SIZE

Quilt: 44" x 52"/112 cm x 130 cm
Block size: 7"/18 cm square
Border block size: $3^1/2$"/9 cm square
Total number of full blocks: 30
Total number of border blocks: 48
Filler strips: 8

FABRIC QUANTITIES

small amounts of assorted fabric for
    the blocks
$3/4$ yd/70 cm of 45"/115 cm wide
    fabric for the narrow borders and
    bindings
$1^2/3$ yds/1.4 m of 45"/115 cm wide
    backing fabric
48" x 56"/120 cm x 140 cm batting

NOTIONS

cardboard or template plastic
pencil and ruler
safety pins, pins, needles and scissors
rotary (Olfa) cutter and mat (optional)
sewing machine
sewing thread

CUTTING

Do not forget to add seam allowances to each piece you cut.

1 Cut templates **a**, **b**, **c** and **d** from firm cardboard or template plastic. Lay the templates on the wrong side of the fabric, aligning the marked or longest edge with the grainline. Trace around the templates, using a soft, sharp pencil. This pencil line will be the sewing line. Cut out with seam allowances.

2 *For each of the 30 blocks:* Cut one **a** piece, four **b** pieces (each from the same fabric), four **c** pieces (each from the same fabric).
  Vary the positions of light, medium and dark-toned fabrics in the blocks for added interest.

3 *For each of the 48 border blocks:* Cut two **c** pieces (in different fabrics). Again, use a variety of light, medium and dark-toned fabrics.

4 *For the filler strips:* Cut eight **d** pieces from medium-toned fabrics.

CONSTRUCTION

5 Sew a **b** piece to each side of an **a** piece. Note that the seam allowance of the **b** piece will extend beyond the side of the **a** piece. Press the seams to one side.

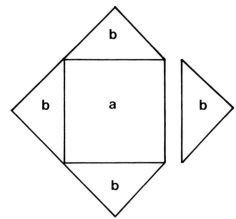

6 Sew a **c** piece to each of the joined **b** sides as illustrated on page 54. Press seams to one side.

53

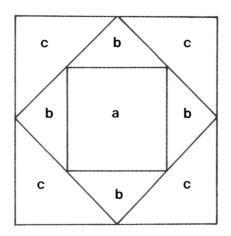

7 Lay out the thirty blocks in a pleasing color arrangement of five rows across and six rows down.

8 Sew each row together, taking care to match the points. Press the seams to one side.

9 Sew the rows together to form the quilt top. Press the seams to one side.

10 Measure down through the center to find the length of the quilt top. Cut two strips of border fabric the same length as this measurement, and 1"/2.5 cm wide plus seam allowances. Join strips, if necessary, to make the length required. Sew these strips to each long side of the quilt

Below: Detail of the quilt

top. Press the seams to one side.

11 Measure across through the center to find the width of the quilt, including the border strips. Cut two strips of border fabric the same length as this measurement, and 1"/2.5 cm wide plus seam allowances. Join strips, if necessary, to make the length required. Sew these strips to the short sides of the quilt top. Press the seams to one side.

12 Piece the border block by sewing two **c** blocks together. Press the seams to one side. Lay out the forty-eight border blocks around the quilt top, taking account of the tonal values and changing the angle of the seam in alternate blocks.

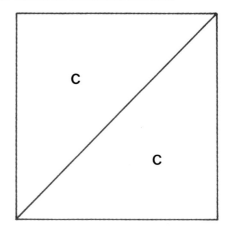

13 Place the filler strips around the corner blocks as illustrated. Join the border blocks into rows with the filler strips and stitch them to the sides of the quilt top. Press quilt top well.

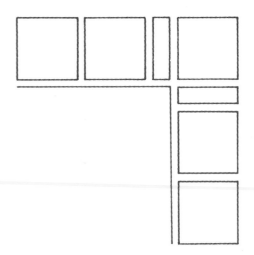

QUILTING

14 Assemble the three layers on a flat surface, placing the backing fabric first face down, then the batting, and finally the quilt top with right side up. Smooth out any wrinkles. Pin-baste the three layers together well with safety pins.

15 Quilt by machine along the seamlines.

FINISHING

16 Trim off any excess batting and backing fabric. Cut two lengths of binding fabric 3$\frac{1}{4}$"/8 cm wide for the quilt sides and two lengths for the top and bottom. Measure, as before, through the center of the quilt to determine the lengths. Press the strips in half, wrong sides together. Place the binding on the right side of the quilt with raw edges even. Stitch in a $\frac{3}{8}$"/1 cm seam. Fold the binding to the wrong side and slipstitch into place.

17 Embroider your name and the date on your quilt.

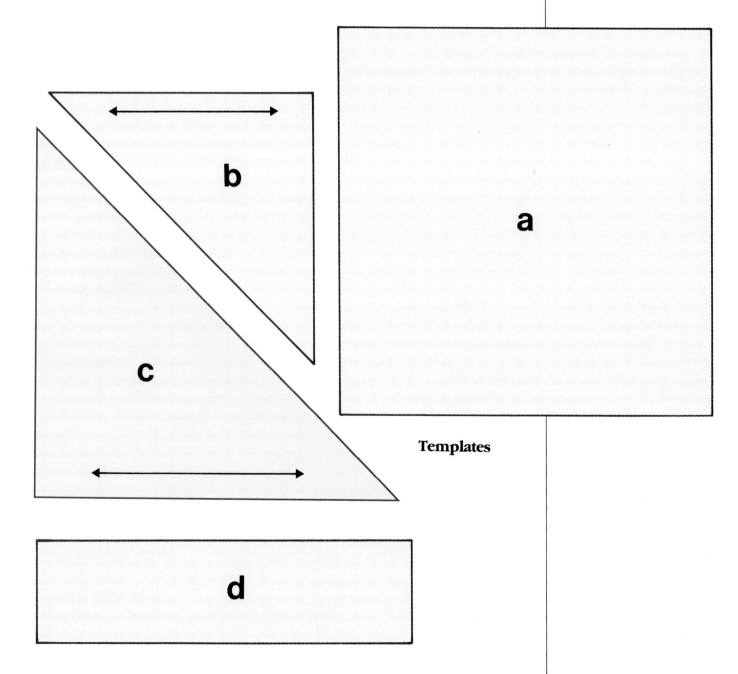

Templates

TRIANGLE WALL QUILT

Colour is crucial in this dazzling quilt, designed and made by Beryl Hodges. This quilt has been machine-pieced and machine-quilted.

FABRIC SUGGESTIONS

Choose four shades to contrast with the black.

FINISHED SIZE

Quilt: 42" x 59"/105 cm x 147 cm

Block size: 4"/10 cm triangle

Total number of full blocks: 207 (103 black and 104 colored)

Total half blocks: 18 (10 black and 8 colored)

FABRIC QUANTITIES

All fabrics are 45"/115 cm wide

$1^{1}/_{8}$ yds/1 m black fabric for the triangles

$1^{1}/_{2}$ yds/1.3 m black fabric for the second border and bindings

$^{1}/_{4}$ yd/20 cm each of four shades of blue

$^{1}/_{4}$ yd/20 cm each of four shades of pink

$^{1}/_{4}$ yd/20 cm each of four shades of green

$^{1}/_{4}$ yd/20 cm each of four shades of purple

$^{1}/_{3}$ yd/30 cm of border fabric (first border)

$1^{2}/_{3}$ yd/1.5 m backing fabric

44" x 60"/110 cm x 150 cm batting

NOTIONS

cardboard or template plastic
pencil and ruler
rotary (Olfa) cutter and mat
safety pins, pins, needles and scissors
sewing machine
sewing thread

CUTTING

Do not forget to add seam allowances to each piece you cut.

1 Cut templates **a** and **b** from firm cardboard or template plastic. Lay the templates on the wrong side of the fabric, with base of triangle along the grainline. Trace around the template with a sharp pencil. Sew on this line. Cut out with seam allowances.

2 Using template **a**, cut: 103 black triangles and 104 colored triangles in the required numbers for each shade as shown in the photo.

3 Using template **b**, cut: 10 black half triangles, and 8 colored half triangles in the required numbers for each shade as shown.

CONSTRUCTION

4 Lay out the black and colored triangles and half triangles as shown in the photo, placing the straight grain of the fabric vertically.

5 Join the triangles together into nine vertical rows, beginning and ending each row with a half triangle. Do not sew past the points. Press the seam allowances to one side.

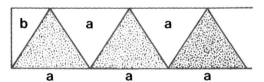

6 Sew the nine horizontal rows together, matching points exactly, to form the quilt top. Press the seam allowances to one side.

7 Measure across the center of the quilt top to determine its width. Cut two 1"/2.5 cm wide strips of the colored border fabric the same length as this measurement. Join strips if necessary to achieve the length required. Sew these strips to each short

Right: The quilt is pictured hanging vertically. To follow the construction instructions, turn the page sideways.

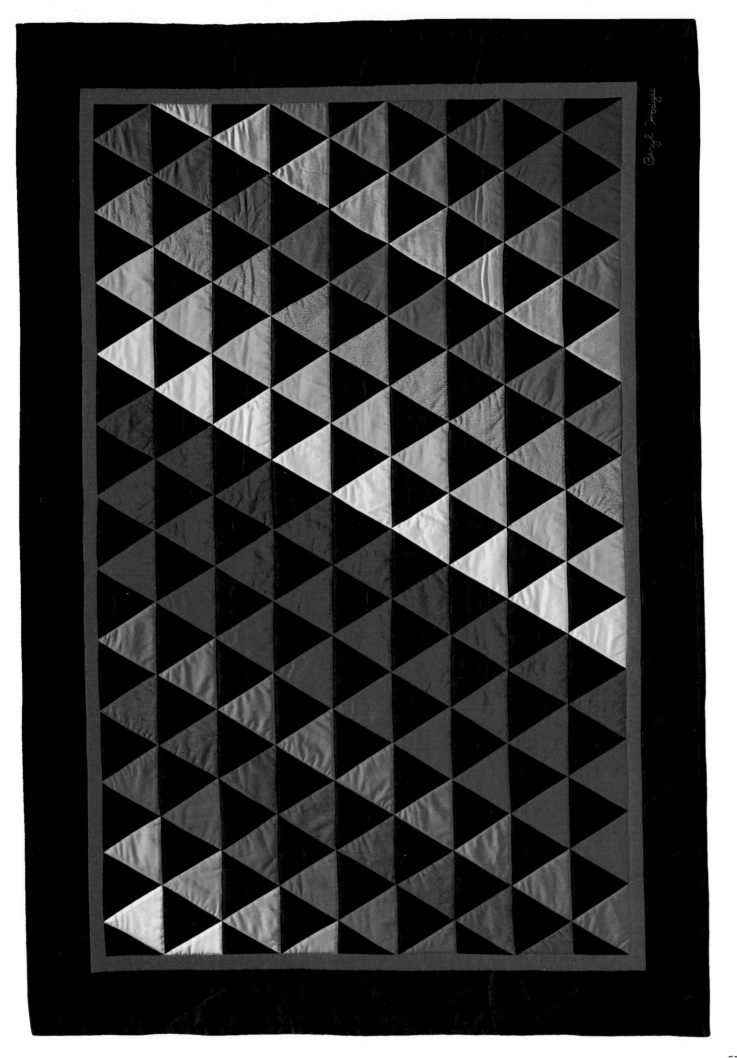

side of the quilt top, taking care to sew exactly at the points of the triangles.

8 Measure down through the center of the quilt top, including the border strips, to find the length. Cut two strips of colored border fabric as for the side borders and attach in the same way.

9 Repeat steps 7 and 8 for the black border, cutting the strips 4"/10 cm wide plus seam allowances. Press the quilt top carefully.

10 Assemble the layers of the quilt on a table with the backing facing down, the batting in between and the quilt top facing upwards. Baste with big stitches or pin-baste through all thicknesses to secure the three layers of the quilt together.

QUILTING

11 Machine-quilt in the seamlines of the triangles and borders, extending the quilting stitching across the borders all the way to the edges.

FINISHING

12 Trim off excess batting and backing. Cut two lengths of $3^1/4"/8$ cm wide black binding for the quilt sides and two lengths for the quilt top and bottom. Measure through the centers, as before, to determine the lengths. Press the strips in half, wrong sides together. Place the binding on the right side of the quilt with raw edges even. Stitch. Fold the binding to the wrong side and slipstitch in place.

13 Sew a sleeve along the top of the quilt back, so that a light dowel can be inserted for hanging. Sign and date your quilt.

Right: Detail of the Triangle Wall Quilt showing the borders and the diagonal quilting

CARE OF QUILTS

Look after your quilt and it will last long enough to become a family heirloom. The enemies are dust, light, humidity and insects. Good housekeeping will help to preserve your quilt and protect it from damage.

Cotton quilts should be washed in your washing machine on a gentle cycle, in warm water, and dried flat in the shade. Quilts should not be exposed to strong light. If you need to store a quilt for long periods, take it out regularly for airing every six months and then fold it in a different way before putting it back into store.

The correct way to fold a quilt when it is not in use, is to fold it with the right side outwards. Then put it into a bag made of well-washed cotton fabric along with rolls of acid-free tissue paper, tucked into the folds. Never store a quilt in a plastic bag as this traps humidity in the enclosed air and causes discoloration. The cotton bag, with the quilt inside, can be put into a cardboard box with mothballs outside the bag to discourage insects.

Most important of all, your quilt was made to be enjoyed for its usefulness and admired for its beauty.

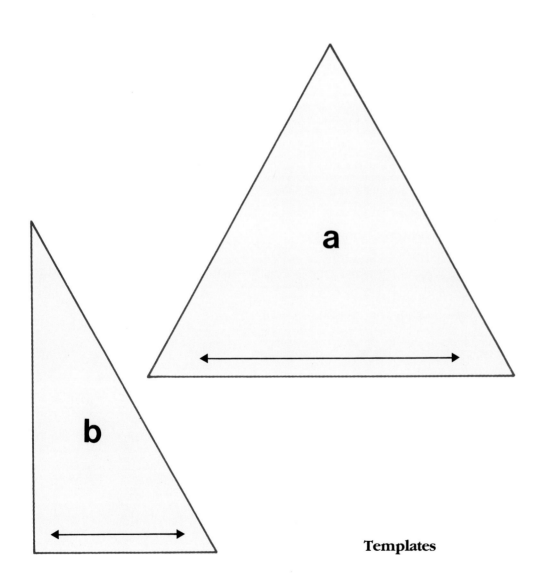

Templates

FLYING GEESE

In this traditional quilt, designed and made by Ann Crafter, the pattern works in parallel lines of triangles along the length of the quilt. It is not difficult to imagine that the triangles are in fact geese flying in formation, with outstretched wings.

FABRIC SUGGESTIONS

The 'sky' triangles are often white or cream and the 'geese' are either in a combination of related colors and fabrics (as in this quilt) or in a single contrasting color. For our quilt we have chosen six different fabrics for the 'geese' – two light, two medium and two dark. The interesting striped sashes are not pieced but are in fact cut from a striped fabric that gives the effect of being pieced from a number of different stripes.

Seam allowances of $^1/4$"/6 mm have been included.

FINISHED SIZE

Quilt: 40" x 48"/103 cm x 124 cm
Block size: 7" x $3^1/2$"/18 cm x 9 cm
Total number of full blocks: 30

FABRIC QUANTITIES

6 different scrap fabrics for the geese
All the following fabrics are 45"/115 cm wide:

1 yd/80 cm light color for the background

$1^1/8$ yds /1 m paisley striped fabric for the sashes

$^2/3$ yd/50 cm dark plain color for border

$^1/2$ yd/40 cm contrasting plain fabric for binding

$1^1/2$ yds /130 cm plain fabric for backing

42" x 50"/110 cm x 130 cm batting

NOTIONS

cardboard or template plastic
pencil and ruler
rotary (Olfa) cutter and mat
safety pins, pins, needles and scissors
sewing thread
sewing machine

CUTTING

1 Cut 4"/10.5 cm wide strips from the six colors of scrap fabric and the light background color. Cut into 4"/10.5 cm lengths to make squares.

2 Cut four sashes from the striped fabric to be approximately $3^1/2$"/9 cm wide and 36"/91.5 cm long.

CONSTRUCTION

3 Place one background square and one print square together with right sides facing and draw a line diagonally from one corner to the other. Sew a line of stitching $^1/4$"/6 mm on either side of this line.

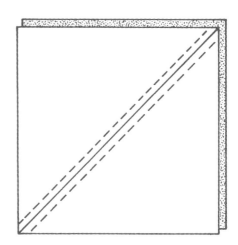

4 Cut along the pencil line, open out the fabric and you will have

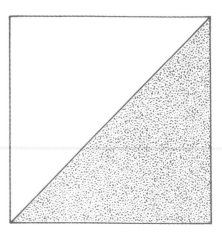

61

two new squares half 'goose' and half background. Sew the 'goose' sides of the squares together, matching print fabrics, to make a rectangular block. Press. Make five of these blocks in each print fabric, making a total of thirty blocks.

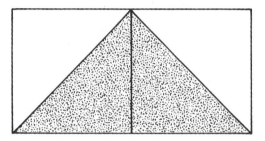

5 Lay the rectangles out in three rows of ten so that you can judge the arrangement of colours and prints. Sew them into three strips. Make sure that the geese are 'flying' in the same direction across the quilt when the strips are laid next to each other. Press.

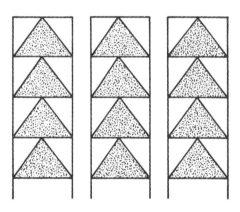

6 Join the three 'geese' strips with striped sashes in between and on the outside, making sure the rectangles are in line. The sashes on the outside form the inner border. Measure across the centre to find the width of the quilt top. Cut two sashes to this width. Sew them to the top and bottom of the quilt top. Press.

7 Measure down the centre of the quilt to find the full length. Cut two outside borders from the plain, dark fabric of this length and 9.5 cm wide. Sew them to the sides of the quilt. Measure through the centre of the quilt top, including the borders just attached, to find the full width. Cut two outer borders to this length and 9.5 cm wide. Sew them to the top and bottom of the quilt top. Press the quilt top carefully.

8 Cut the backing fabric to size and place it right side down. If you can fit it on a table, sticky tape it to the table to stop it from slipping. Place the batting over the backing and the pieced quilt top over this, with the right side up. Smooth out any wrinkles and, using safety pins, pin the three layers together all over the quilt.

QUILTING

9 Starting in the middle of the quilt (using a walking foot, if you have one) stitch around the 'geese' triangles first.

TIP

It's a good idea to do the quilting in zigzag lines, working down only one side of each 'goose' from top to bottom, and then stitching the other side from top to bottom. This means you can work in continuous rows without too much starting and stopping in your sewing.

10 Stitch across the striped borders with parallel rows of stitching, approximately 1"/3 cm apart. Take care to mark this out first so you end up with even rows at the corners. The plain dark border and the sashes are quilted with joined ovals, the pattern for which is given opposite. Trace the design and make a template for your stitching. Transfer the design to your fabric, using a silver pencil or a water-soluble pencil. Trim off any excess backing and batting.

FINISHING

11 Measure through the center of the quilt lengthwise and cross-wise as before to determine the lengths of the binding strips. Cut the binding $3^{1}/4"/8$ cm wide. Press the binding strips in half, wrong sides together. Stitch the binding to the right side of the quilt with raw edges even. Turn the binding to the wrong side of the quilt and slipstitch it into place.

Above: Detail of quilt showing the border, sashes and quilting

Quilting design

Evening Star

Designed and made by Lee Cleland, this large quilt is made up of two blocks, Evening Star and Dutch Tile. This quilt has been machine-pieced and machine-quilted.

Evening Star block

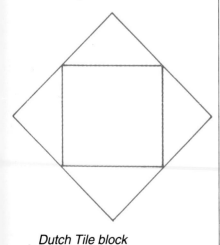

Dutch Tile block

FABRIC SUGGESTIONS

Choose a light fabric for the background of the stars; a medium one for the triangles of the Dutch Tile block and side triangles; a medium to dark fabric for the points of the star, the center square of Dutch Tile and the first border; choose a darker fabric for the center of the star and the outside border. The blocks are set diagonally.

FINISHED SIZE

Quilt: 85" x 99"/210 cm x 250 cm
Block size: $10^{1}/4$"/25.5 cm square
Total number of blocks:
    30 Evening Star
    20 Dutch Tile

FABRIC QUANTITIES

All fabrics are 45"/115 cm wide.
$3^{1}/3$ yds/3 m light fabric
$2^{7}/8$ yds/2.5 m medium fabric
$4^{1}/4$ yds/3.7 m medium to dark fabric
3 yds/2.6 m dark fabric
89" x 103"/220 cm x 260 cm backing fabric (pieced from 6 yds/5.2 m fabric)
89" x 103"/220 cm x 260 cm batting

NOTIONS

cardboard or template plastic
water-soluble pencil or silver pencil
ruler
tracing paper
rotary (Olfa) cutter and mat (optional)
safety pins, needles and scissors
sewing thread
sewing machine

CUTTING

See pages 68 and 69 for the templates. Add $^{1}/4$"/6 mm seam allowances to all the pieces you cut except for the side triangles which already include $^{1}/4$"/6 mm seam allowances.

1 Make templates **1a**, **1b**, **1c**, **2a**, **2b**, **2c** from cardboard. Using a sharp pencil, trace around the templates on the wrong side of the fabric. Cut them out, adding seam allowances. The pencil line will be your sewing line. Cut the pieces for the blocks along the length of the fabric to allow you to cut the borders along the length later.

For the Dutch Tile block: Cut,
20 squares (template **1a**) medium to dark fabric
80 triangles (template **2a**) medium fabric
For the Evening Star block: Cut,
30 squares (template **1b**) dark fabric
240 triangles (template **2c**) medium to dark fabric
120 triangles (template **2b**) light fabric
120 squares (template **1c**) light fabric
For the side triangles: Cut five 15"/ 37 cm squares of light fabric and cut them diagonally through the center into four triangles. NOTE: These side triangles <u>include</u> seam allowances.
For the corner triangles: Cut four of template **2d** of light fabric.

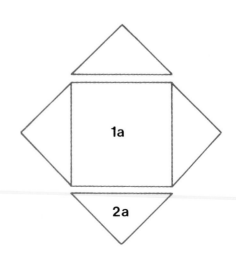

64

65

CONSTRUCTION

For the Dutch Tile blocks:

2 Join the long side of a triangle **2a** to each side of the square **1a** in a $1/4"$/6 mm seam. Press this and all following seams to one side.

For the Evening Star blocks:

3 Join a triangle **2c** to each short side of a triangle **2b** to form Strip 1. Press.

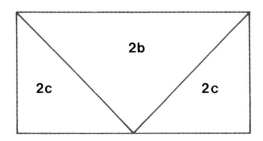

4 Sew a Strip 1 to two opposite sides of a square **1b**. Press.

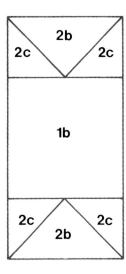

5 Make two more Strip 1 pieces. On each one, join a square **1c** to the other short side of the triangle **2c** to form Strip 2. Press.

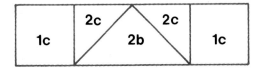

6 Sew a Strip 2 to opposite sides of the square **1b** to complete the block. Press.

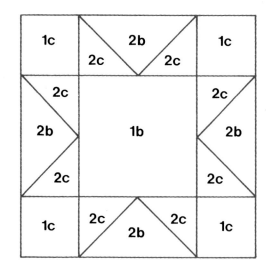

7 Arrange the blocks as shown in the photo, adding the corner and side triangles to the diagonal rows. Sew together in rows, then sew the rows together.

8 *For the borders:* Measure the width of the quilt top through the center and then the length through the center (allowing for the width of the top and bottom borders) to find the length required for the borders. Add an extra 16"/40 cm to each one to allow for the mitered corners. From the medium to dark fabric, cut the strips for the inner border $2^{3}/4"$/7 cm wide plus seam allowances. From the dark fabric, cut strips for the second border 4"/10 cm wide plus seam allowances. Sew both strips together for each border, making a wide, striped border. Sew these to the top, bottom and sides of the quilt, stopping the stitching short of the seam allowances of the quilt top at the corners. Fold the quilt at the corners, so that the edges of the borders are matching and stitch the corners of the borders together in a line with the fold in the quilt to form a mitered corner.

9 Trace the quilting patterns from pages 70 and 71. Make a template from the cardboard or plastic. Using the template, a silver pencil or water-

soluble pencil, draw the designs onto the quilt top. Use the circle for the *Dutch Tile* blocks, the flower for the center square of the *Evening Star* block, the corner triangles and the side triangles, and the border pattern, including the corner pattern, for the quilt border.

10 Place the three layers of the quilt together – backing right side facing down, batting on top and then the quilt top with the right side up. Pin-baste through all thicknesses.

QUILTING

11 Quilt by machine along the pattern lines.

FINISHING

12 *For the binding*: Cut two lengths of dark fabric $3^1/4''/$ 8 cm wide plus seam allowances for the quilt sides and two lengths the same width for the top and bottom. Measure through the center of the quilt as before to determine the lengths of binding required. Press the binding in half, wrong sides together and raw edges even. Lay the binding on the right side of the quilt with raw edges together and stitch in a $^3/8''/$ 1 cm seam. Fold the pressed edge to the wrong side and slipstitch into place.

Left: Detail of the Evening Star quilt showing the dainty quilting designs

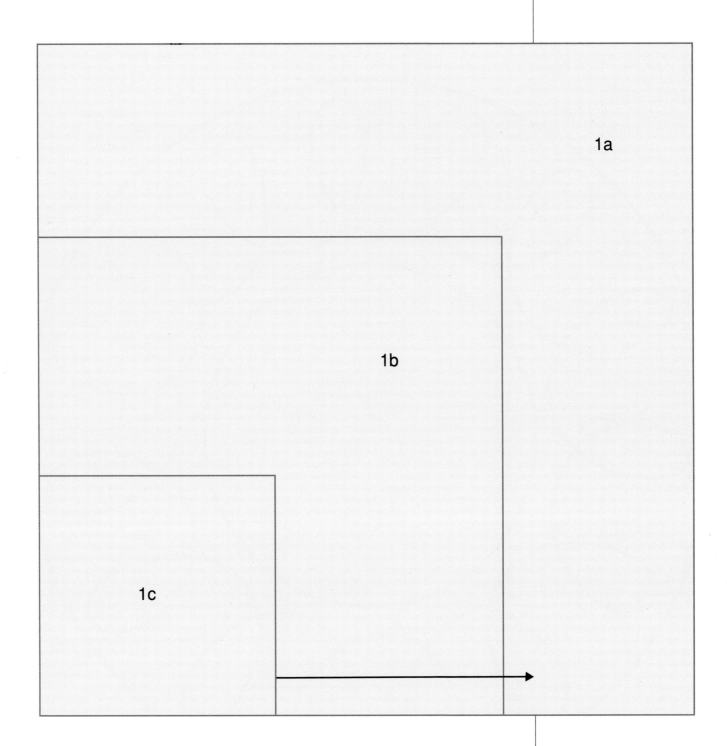

1a

1b

1c

Templates

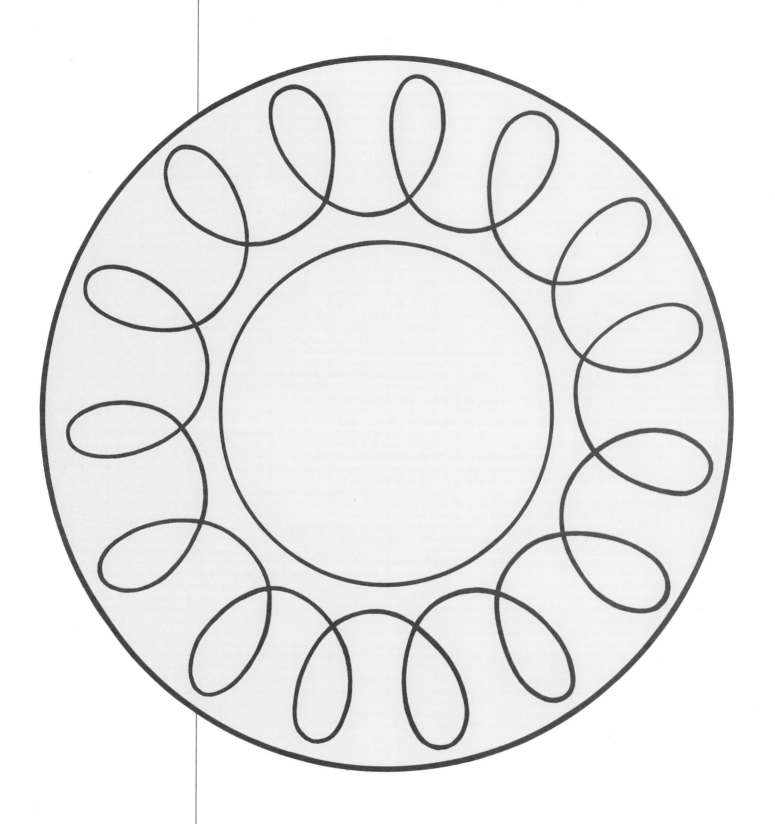

GARDEN PATH

*Lynette McKinley,
designer and
quiltmaker, chose a
lush floral print to
combine with a strong
geometric pattern. The
quilt has been
machine-pieced and
machine-quilted.*

FABRIC SUGGESTIONS

For added interest, the floral design
works in striped panels and the triangular template **c** has been cut from
different parts of the stripe. This process does involve a lot of waste so you
will need to be generous when buying
fabric. The quilt, which has been made
using six each of two blocks, can be
enlarged by adding more blocks.

$1/4$"/6 mm seam allowances are
included.

FINISHED SIZE

Quilt: 48" x 60"/119 cm x 150 cm
Block size: $12^1/2$"/31 cm square
Total number of full blocks: 12

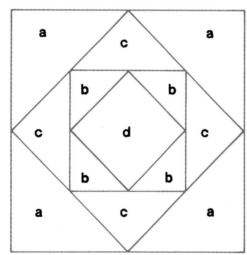

Block 1

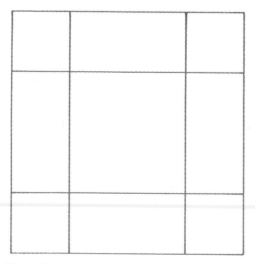

Block 2

FABRIC QUANTITIES

$1^1/4$ yds/1 m (approximately) of
striped floral fabric
$2/3$ yd/60 cm blue fabric for small
triangles
$3/4$ yd/70 cm cream fabric for large
triangles and blocks
$1/4$ yd/20 cm red print fabric
$1/2$ yd/40 cm solid red fabric
2 yds/1.6 m striped fabric for borders
$3^1/2$ yds/3.1 m of 45"/115 cm wide
backing fabric pieced to make
49" x 62"/125 cm x 155 cm (if you
have a crosswise seam in the backing you can reduce this to $2^3/4$ yds/
2.5 m)
49" x 62"/125 cm x 155 cm batting

NOTIONS

template plastic
pencil and ruler
rotary (Olfa) cutter and mat
safety pins, pins, needles and scissors
sewing thread and quilting thread
sewing machine

CUTTING

See pages 76 and 77 for the
templates.
For Block 1:

1 Cut the four templates out of
transparent plastic so you can
plan the placement of the fabric
pattern. Cut template **d** six times out of
the center roses, placing each one the
same way on the fabric.

2 Fold the blue fabric in half and
then fold it again so you have four
layers. After straightening the edge and

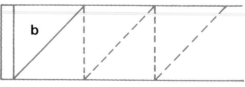

↑ *Cut off selvage*

72

cutting off the selvages, cut a strip 4"/ 10 cm wide using scissors or a rotary cutter and plastic ruler. Lay template **b** along the strip as shown and cut out twenty-four triangles.

3 The next triangles, **c**, are cut individually from the striped material. Lay the see-through template down over a particular stripe and cut four triangles the same from each section for each of the six blocks.

4 From the cream fabric, cut two strips across the width of the fabric each 7"/17 cm wide. Cut twenty-four triangles from the cream fabric using template **a**.

For Block 2:
5 Folding it into four as for the blue fabric, cut two 3¹/2"/9 cm wide strips across the width of the floral fabric. Cut one 7"/16.5 cm wide strip across the cream solid fabric. Cut two 3¹/2"/9 cm wide and one 7"/16.5 cm wide strips from the solid red fabric.

CONSTRUCTION
6 *To make Block 1:* Sew the long side of a blue triangle to all four sides of the small floral square cut

from template **d**. They should extend beyond the corners of the square to allow the next triangle to go on without losing the corner of the square.

7 Join four striped triangles to the sides of the square and then sew on four plain cream triangles. Make five more of these blocks. Press all the blocks carefully.

8 *To make Block 2:* Join the two floral strips across their width with the one 7"/16.5 cm wide plain red strip in between.

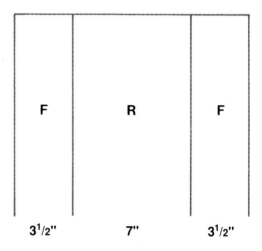

9 Press the seams to one side and cut the joined strip into strips 3¹/2"/9 cm wide.

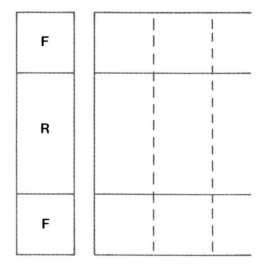

10 Join the remaining red strips to the cream strip in the same way. Press the seams to one side and cut into strips 7"/16.5 cm wide. Piece

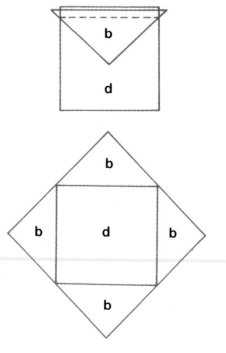

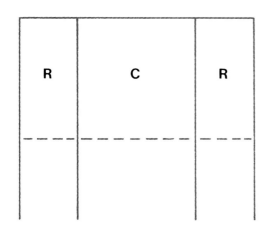

R	C	R

two strips with the floral squares on both ends to two opposite sides of the plain red and cream strip. Make five more of these blocks. Press all blocks carefully.

F	R	F
R	C	R
F	R	F

11 Piece the quilt together, alternating blocks and matching corners carefully. Sew in rows, first Block 1, then Block 2, then Block 1. In the second row, join Block 2, Block 1, then Block 2. For the third row, join Block 1, then Block 2, then Block 1 and so on. Continue until the quilt is finished.

12 Measure the width of the quilt through the centre. Cut the border from the striped fabric to this length, using whatever width best complements your stripes. Join the borders to the top and bottom of the quilt. Press. Repeat for the border on the sides of the quilt.

QUILTING

13 Place the backing fabric face down on a table and sticky tape it to the table to prevent it slipping. Place the batting on top and then the pieced quilt top on top of that, face up. Carefully smooth out all the wrinkles. Using large safety pins and starting in the middle of the quilt, pin all three layers together. Machine-quilt, or hand-quilt if you prefer, the complete top with crisscrossing diagonal rows of stitching, about $2^1/2"/6$ cm apart. Trim off any excess backing and batting.

FINISHING

14 Cut $3^1/4"/8$ cm wide strips from the solid red fabric for the binding. Measure across the center of the quilt to find the length and width to calculate the length of binding required. The edges of a quilt are sometimes stretched and it may ripple along the edges and not sit straight, making accurate measurement a problem. Fold the binding strip in half, wrong sides together and raw edges matching. Sew to the top and bottom edges of the quilt, stretching the binding to fit along the edges. Sew the rest to both sides of the quilt. Fold to the back of the quilt and slipstitch in place.

KEY		
R	=	RED
C	=	CREAM
F	=	FLORAL

Below: Detail of the Garden Path quilt showing the crisscrossing machine quillting

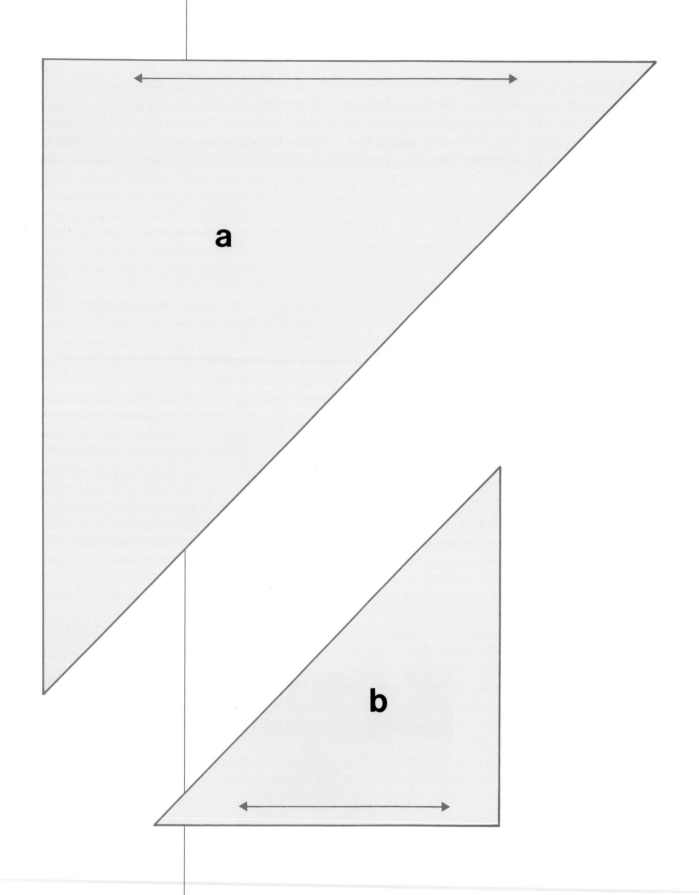

a

b

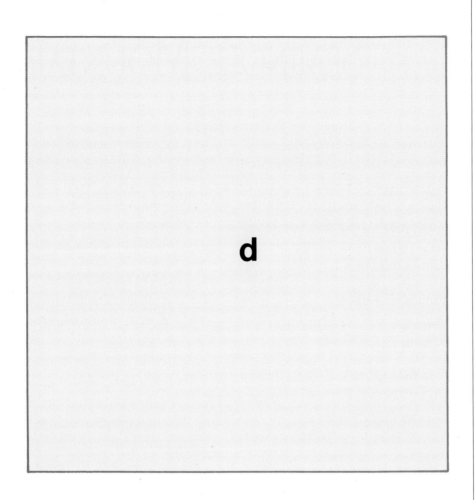

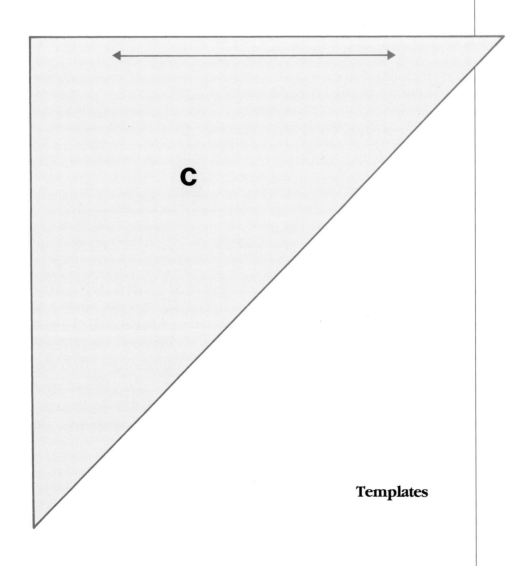

Templates

Seminole Mountain

This charming quilt, designed and made by Sandy Mann, is a combination of traditional quilting designs. It is very important, to measure and cut this quilt accurately, and to be accurate with the ³/₈"/1 cm seam allowance.

FABRIC SUGGESTIONS

Seminole patterns involve joining strips of patches, often in very bright colors, which are then cut up before being joined into new combinations. This quilt is made by the chain sewing method which is a great time saver.

FINISHED SIZE

Quilt: 38" x 60"/96 cm x 154 cm
Squares: 2¹/₃"/6 cm

FABRIC QUANTITIES

1 yd/90 cm of 45"/115 cm wide green print fabric
³/₄ yd/70 cm of 45"/115 cm wide cream print fabric
¹/₄ yd/20 cm of 45"/115 cm wide coral print fabric
⁷/₈ yd/80 cm of 45"/115 cm solid cream fabric
³/₄ yd/65 cm solid coral fabric for borders
1³/₄ yds/1.6 m solid coral backing fabric
42" x 64"/115 cm x 160 cm batting

NOTIONS

cardboard or template plastic
pencils and ruler
rotary (Olfa) cutter and mat
safety pins, pins, needles and scissors
sewing thread
sewing machine

CUTTING

1 The triangular template includes seam allowances. Use it to cut out in the following quantities: 130 green print, 146 cream print, 24 coral print.

2 Cut three 3¹/₈"/8 cm wide strips of green print and six 3¹/₈"/8 cm wide strips of plain coral for the Seminole strips.

3 Before cutting the borders, it is best to measure the length and width of the main panel, measuring through the center. Join fabric as necessary to achieve the lengths required for border strips.

CONSTRUCTION

4 Chainsew the following combination of triangles together into squares. Do not cut them apart, but feed in one pair of patches after another and sew them all at once. 8 green print triangles into 4 squares 124 green print triangles and 124 cream print triangles into 124 squares; 24 coral print triangles and 24 cream print triangles into 24 squares. Cut the threads between patches and press the seams to one side.

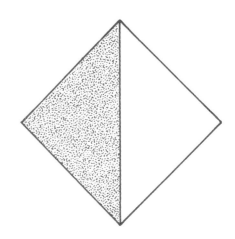

5 Sew the squares into strips following the diagram provided on the next page, for placement of the various colors. It is important when sewing the joined patches together, to match the cross seams. Pin them together as shown, stitch and press the seams to one side. Continue in this manner.

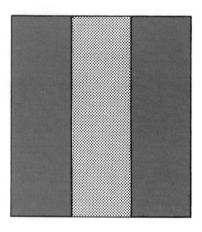

center. Join them to the side edges of the panel. (Fig. 2)

10 Measure the quilt top as in Step 6 and cut and attach the $3^1/8$"/8 cm wide cream and coral plain borders as for the inner borders, sewing the top and bottom borders first and then the sides.

11 *For the Seminole strips:* Join the green print strips between two plain coral strips. Press the seams open. Cut the joined strip crosswise into $3^1/8$"/8 cm lengths.

Pin and sew the lengths together in an offset pattern as shown in the diagram below. Press the seams open. Trim diagonally through the coral squares, allowing for seam allowances.

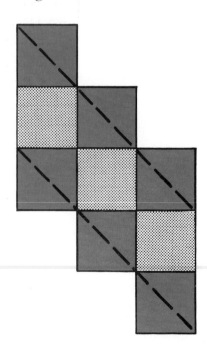

6 Measure the width of the panel through the center and cut two plain coral borders $1^3/4$"/4.5 cm wide and as long as this length. Sew these strips to the top and bottom of the center panel. Measure the length of the quilt, including the coral border, and cut two $1^3/4$"/4.5 cm wide plain coral borders for the sides. Sew them to both sides of the center panel.

7 Measure the quilt top as in Step 6. Cut and sew $2^1/8$"/5.5 cm wide plain cream borders for the top, bottom and sides.

8 Make four strips, each with ten green and cream print squares, noting that the direction of the seams changes in the center. Join strips together in pairs and join to the top and bottom edges of the panel. (Fig. 1)

9 Make two strips, each with sixteen green and cream print squares, noting the change of direction of the seams at the ends and in the

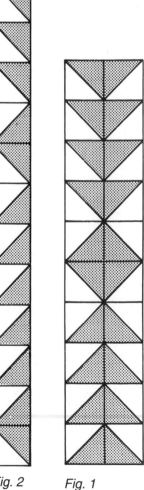

Fig. 2   *Fig. 1*

12 Measure the width of the quilt top through the center. Sew the Seminole strips of this measurement to the top and bottom of the quilt.

13 Measure the width of the quilt top through the center and cut and add another $3^{1}/8$"/8 cm cream border to the top and bottom of the quilt. Press the quilt top carefully.

QUILTING

14 Pencil mark your quilting design on the borders, meeting edges and points where possible.

15 Assemble quilt layers, placing the backing face down on a table, then the batting and finally the quilt top, face up. Pin-baste together with safety pins. Machine-quilt along seamlines and in the marked pattern on the borders.

16 *For the mock binding*: Machine sew or tack around the edge of the quilt. Trim the batting around the edges. Trim the backing to be 1" wider all around each edge.

17 Fold the corner of the backing in half and then over again onto the top of the quilt. Press under the raw edge of the binding all around the quilt and fold the edge onto the front of the quilt. Pin the binding in place, folding in and cutting away the excess fabric at the corners, forming mitered corners. Slipstitch the corners closed. Stitch the folded edge of the binding down onto the quilt front.

Above: Detail of the Seminole Mountain quilt showing the pieced borders

KEY

= YELLOW

= GREEN

= CORAL

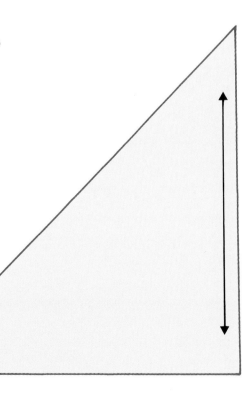

Template

SCRAP BAG QUILT

Kate McEwen and Anne Crafter are responsible for this charming quilt. Traditionally, scrap bag quilts are just that – made by piecing together tiny scraps of printed cotton. This pinwheel design is typical of the scrap bag quilts of the 1930s where the colored scraps were combined with large areas of white fabric which came from old bedsheets.

FABRIC SUGGESTIONS

The scraps in this quilt actually come from a manufacturer's coordinated range of quilting fabrics, Marcus Brothers' Aunt Grace's Scrap Bag, but you can easily use the contents of your scrap bag. Using large areas of white allows you to combine a variety of colored prints, providing you pay attention to the intensity of the colors.

FINISHED SIZE

Quilt: 80" x 60"/186 cm x 136 cm
Block size: 9"/23 cm square
Total number of full blocks: 24

FABRIC QUANTITIES

40"/1 m of a variety of cotton print scraps
4 yds/3.5 m white fabric
2 yds/1.7 m print fabric for the borders
28"/70 cm print fabric for the binding
84" x 64"/196 cm x 146 cm cotton fabric for the backing (pieced from 5 yds/230 cm of 36"/90 cm wide fabric)
84" x 64"/196 cm x 146 cm batting

NOTIONS

rotary (Olfa) cutter and mat
plastic ruler
safety pins, pins, needles and scissors
sewing thread
sewing machine

CUTTING

1/4"/6 mm allowances are included in the cutting instructions.

1 For each of the twelve pinwheel blocks, cut eight triangles using template **a** from scrap fabrics, four triangles using template **b** and four strips using template **c** from white fabric.

2 Cut approximately seventy-four triangles from scrap fabric, using template **d** for the borders.

CONSTRUCTION

3 For the pinwheel blocks, join each of forty-eight scrap triangles (template **a**) to one of the forty-eight white triangles (template **b**).

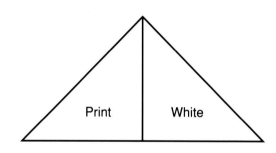

4 Join the remaining forty-eight scrap triangles (template **a**) to the white strips to make a large triangle.

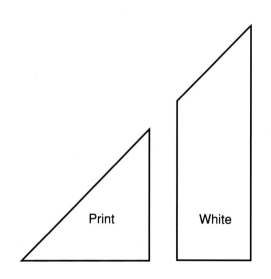

5 Join pairs of the large triangles made in steps 3 and 4 to form squares.

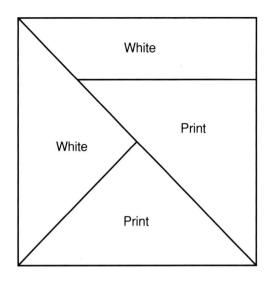

6 Join four squares together to make the pinwheel block. Take care to line up the points carefully at the center of the pinwheel.

7 Measure the size of your block and cut plain white squares to this size. They should be approximately $9^1/2"$/24 cm square.

8 Join the blocks together, alternating plain blocks with pinwheel blocks, and setting the blocks four across and six down. Press.

9 Measure the length of the quilt top, measuring through the center. Cut two 3"/8 cm wide white strips to this length plus seam allowances. Sew these to the sides of the quilt top.

10 Measure the width of the quilt, measuring through the center and including the white border just sewn on. Cut two 3"/8 cm wide white strips to this length plus seam allowances. Sew these to the top and bottom of the quilt top. Press.

11 Join each of the scrap triangles for the border to each of the white triangles to form squares. Join the squares together to form the middle border, placing a small white square at each corner.

12 Measure the quilt top through the center as before and cut four 4"/10 cm wide strips from the print border fabric. Join the borders to the quilt top. Press.

13 Piece the backing fabric to achieve the correct size.

QUILTING

14 Using cardboard or template plastic, trace and cut out the template for the quilting. Mark the quilting design onto the center of each white square.

15 Lay the backing fabric, face down, on a table. Place the batting on top and the quilt top on top of that, face up. Baste or pin-baste with safety pins, joining all the layers.

16 Hand-quilt the design on the white square. The white inner border has been machine-quilted in a diamond pattern.

17 Trim off any excess batting and backing.

FINISHING

18 Measure the width and length of the quilt as before and cut 3"/8 cm wide strips for the binding to this length plus seam allowances. Fold the strips in half, wrong sides together. Place binding along the sides of the quilt with right sides together and raw edges even. Stitch. Turn the folded edge to the wrong side and slipstitch into place. Repeat for the top and bottom bindings, finishing the corners neatly.

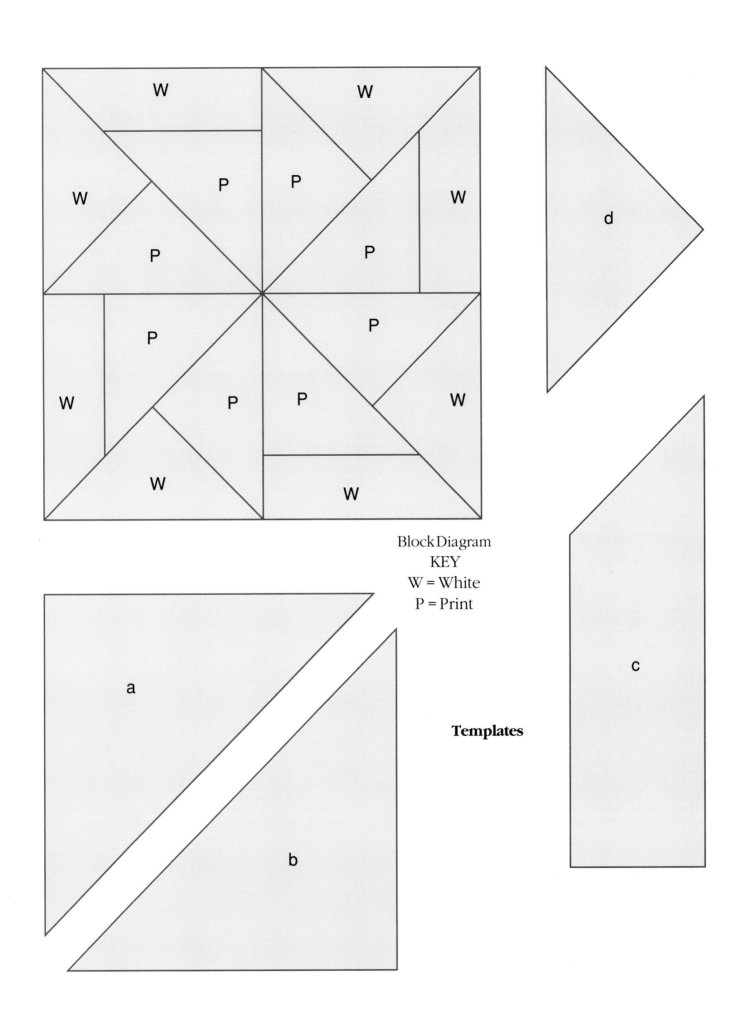

Block Diagram
KEY
W = White
P = Print

Templates

Quilting Diagram

Template

Commuting from Manly *is one of*
Trudy Billingsley's wonderful quilts

Pieces of Pie

This attractive quilt, by Lessa Siegele, can be quickly and easily created using a border print fabric and a 9° wedge ruler. The cuts made using this ruler will produce two different wedges, one up and one down.

FABRIC SUGGESTIONS
Choose a cotton fabric with a strong border design. The quantities given will give you two different circles. Keep one for yourself and have one to give away, or make the second one the beginning of a medallion quilt.

FINISHED SIZE
Quilt: 50"/130 cm in diameter

FABRIC QUANTITIES
5^1/2 yds/5 m of border print fabric
55"/142 cm square of batting
55"/142 cm square of cotton fabric for the backing (pieced from 3 yds/2.8 m fabric)
NOTIONS
rotary (Olfa) cutter and mat
9° wedge ruler
pencil
sewing thread
sewing machine

CUTTING
1 To make the chevron peaks in the quilt, place the wedge ruler on the border print, with the 45° marking on the ruler lined up at exactly the same place each time. You will need two sets of wedges cut at opposite 45° angles. Pair up opposite angle wedges to form the chevron.

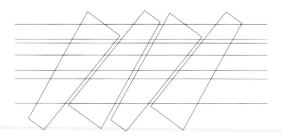

To make sure you always make the cut at the same place, choose a distinctive area in the fabric and add a piece of masking tape to your ruler. Each time you make a cut, ensure that the piece of masking tape falls in exactly the same place. This is important if you are to get the stripes to meet in the finished quilt. It may mean two pieces of tape: one for the up position of the wedge, the other for the down position.

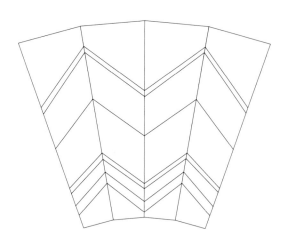

2 Fold the fabric, selvage to selvage, carefully lining up the pattern so that you have exactly the same stripes lined up on the top and the bottom. Make two cuts at once and this will automatically give you both angles for the chevron.

3 With the 9° ruler, you will need forty wedges to complete your circle. Cut twenty wedges in each direction if you are using the fabric doubled. This will give you eighty wedges – enough for two circles.

CONSTRUCTION

4 Divide the cut wedges into two piles, those cut with the wide end of the wedge at the top of the fabric in one pile and those cut with the wide end of the wedge at the bottom in another pile. Select one pile for one circle and the other for another circle.

5 When sewing the wedges together, it is very important to sew the same size seam from one end of the wedge to the other so that the circle lies very flat when finished. It is not essential to have a $1/4$"/6 mm seam allowance but it must be the same width at all times.

6 Sew the wedges together in groups of ten to give you four quarters. This is a good time to line up these quarters on your gridded cutting board to check for accuracy. If the angle is slightly out, trim the quarters to form an exact 90° angle. Make this check after sewing the first ten wedges together. If there is a lot of error, it means adjusting the seams on the first quarter and being more careful when sewing the remaining seams. A piece of tape stuck to the throat plate of your sewing machine will help you sew an even width.

7 When all the wedges are sewn together, there will be a hole in the center approximately 6"/15 cm in diameter. The size will vary slightly from person to person, depending on the size of the seam. Appliqué a circle of fabric to the middle of the piece. Press the quilt top carefully.

8 Cut the lining and batting to be 2"/5 cm bigger all around than the quilt top.

QUILTING

9 Place the quilt top face down on a table. Place the batting on top and

the backing fabric on top of that, face upwards.

10 Baste or pin-baste through all the layers.

11 Machine-quilt along the seam lines. Trim away any excess batting and backing fabric.

12 Cut a strip of 2"/4 cm wide bias strip of fabric for the

binding; piece strips if necessary to achieve the desired length. Fold the strip over double with wrong sides together. Stitch the binding around the edge of the quilt with right sides facing and raw edges even. Turn the folded edge of the binding to the wrong side of the quilt and slipstitch it into place.

Close up of the arrangement of wedges in the quilt

Quick Quilts

*T*he passing of time changes everything, and perhaps nowhere more than in the way homes are furnished with individual creativity. The very best traditional ideas and techniques are shown here, adapted for contemporary projects. They're all simple to make, effective, pretty and practical.

SILK NURSERY QUILT

This delightful nursery quilt is as soft as silk. The pretty nursery designs were first painted by Annie Ubeda, then the quilt was machine-sewn and machine-quilted by Martina Oprey.

FABRIC SUGGESTIONS

China silk is the ideal fabric to use for this quilt because it is nearly transparent, making it easy to trace the designs onto it, and it takes the dye beautifully. There are many paints and dyes available; if you choose a different brand, refer to the manufacturer's directions to choose a suitable fabric.

FINISHED SIZE

Quilt: 40"/1 m square

FABRIC QUANTITIES

40"/1 m square China silk
44"/1.10 m square cotton or silk for backing
44"/1.10 m square polyester batting

NOTIONS AND PAINTS

permanent-ink brown fabric marking pen
Fabric Dye by Delta/Shiva: orange, yellow, pale blue, deep blue, moss green, brown, red, gray, white
Color Resist for fabrics by Delta/Shiva
soft, washable pencil
masking tape
large wooden frame of the size of the silk to be painted
push pins, safety pins
assorted soft-bristle paintbrushes
sewing machine

PAINTING METHOD

See the motif outlines on pages 97, 98 and 99.

1 Mark the silk with a washable pencil: Find the center of the fabric. Center a 9"/22.5 cm square on it. Allowing 2^1/2"/6.5 cm wide borders between them, mark eight more squares as shown in the photo. The outer borders will start wider but will be the same width when the quilt is bound.

2 Center the marked squares over the motifs and trace off the designs using the permanent-ink fabric marking pen. The silk is so transparent that the design will easily be seen through it. Use adhesive tape to hold the silk in place.

3 Stretch the silk onto the wooden frame, securing it with push pins and making sure that the silk is taut. Draw over the design lines with the Color Resist. This forms a barrier, keeping the color in the area where it is intended to be. Do this carefully, without leaving any gaps. A broken line will allow the color to run through. Apply the resist to the border edges as well. The resist dries very quickly, so you do not have to wait too long before you start painting.

4 Test the dye colors on a scrap of fabric, mix or dilute them as desired. These colors are just a guide. Use your own colors if you wish. Paint the motifs, then paint the borders to complement your colors if desired.

5 Let the painted silk dry completely. Following the manufacturer's directions, set the dye and wash out the resist.

CONSTRUCTION

6 Place the backing fabric face down on a table. Tape it to the table to keep it from slipping. Place the batting over it and then the painted silk, face up. Baste these three layers together.

QUILTING

7 Machine-quilt along the painted border lines. Make a line of stitching to define the outer border $2^1/2"/6.5$ cm from the squares.

FINISHING

8 When the quilting is complete, trim batting and silk, $1"/2$ cm beyond the outer stitching, leaving the backing fabric protruding. Trim the backing fabric so that it extends $1^1/4"/3$ cm all round the quilt top.

9 Fold the backing fabric border over the edge of the silk, turning under $^1/2"/1$ cm at the raw edge. Fold in the corners diagonally to create miters. Slipstitch the folded edge of the false binding to the stitching at the edge of the outer painted border.

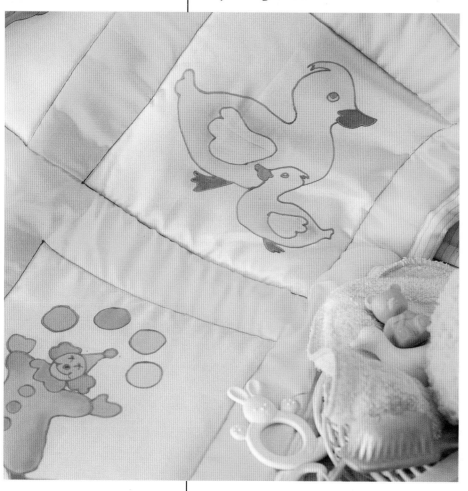

Above: Detail of the Silk Nursery Quilt

Template

Template

Template

MAGIC QUILT

This magic quilt folds up and tucks into a sewn-on pocket, making a pillow! Every sofa needs pillows and something warm to snuggle into – how convenient to unwrap the pillow and find a cuddly quilt inside!

FABRIC SUGGESTIONS

Choose preprinted pillow panels, with one extra panel for the pocket into which the quilt folds. The pocket on the back of the quilt needs to have at least one side in the same fabric as the quilt back. The exact measurements for the quilt will depend upon the proportion of your preprinted fabric – be sure to use a full repeat of the pattern. The pocket should be the size of one preprinted block.

FINISHED SIZE

Quilt: 47" x 67"/118 cm x 162 cm
Pocket: 17"/42 cm square

FABRIC QUANTITIES

2 yds/1.7 m of 48 "/120 cm wide fabric
    for the quilt top
2 yds/1.7 m of 48"/120 cm wide fabric
    for the quilt back
18"/46 cm square each for the pocket
    front and back
48" x 68"/120 cm x 170 cm batting for
    the quilt
18"/46 cm square batting for the
    pocket

NOTIONS

sewing thread
safety pins, pins
sewing machine

CUTTING

$^1/2$"/6 mm allowances are included in the cutting instructions

1 Cut out one quilt front, one quilt back and two pocket pieces in the sizes given.

CONSTRUCTION

2 With the right side facing upwards, place the quilt front over the batting. Pin-baste to secure.

3 With the right side facing upwards, place the pocket front over the batting. Pin-baste to secure. Place the pocket back over the front, with right sides together. Stitch around all the edges in a $^1/2$" seam, leaving an opening for turning.

4 Turn the pocket to the right side and slipstitch the opening closed. Press. Machine-quilt through all thicknesses, following any lines on the front you wish to emphasize.

5 Place the pocket on the back of the quilt in the center of one short end, $^1/2$"/1 cm in from the end. Stitch the pillow in place around three sides, with the opening facing the middle of the quilt. If you have used two coordinating fabrics, make sure the fabric that matches the back is facing upwards when you are positioning the pocket.

6 Place the quilt back over the quilt front, with right sides facing. Stitch around all the edges, leaving an opening for turning.

7 Turn the quilt right side out; press. Slipstitch the opening closed. Tie the quilt through all layers where the 'blocks' intersect.

Above right: The magic quilt opened out
Right: Hand-quilt around the motifs for a different look
Far right: The magic quilt folds into the pillow

To fold the quilt: Place the quilt with the pocket face down and fold in both sides to cross over in the middle. Beginning at the end with no pocket, fold the quilt in pocketsized lengths up to the pocket. Bring the pocket from the back to the front, turning it to contain the folded quilt.

PILLOW QUILT

Tonia Todman designed the arrangement of colours and patterns for this quilt. The quilt can be any size you like, depending on the number and size of the squares. Martina Oprey used an overlocker to join the squares together and speed up construction.

FABRIC SUGGESTIONS

The construction method of this quilt lends itself to creating a design using different related fabrics. We've chosen a range of prints in blue and white, but this quilt would be just as eye-catching using solid fabrics in pastels or primary colors. It could even become a 'memory' quilt by using scraps from the children's clothes or your favorite dresses. Experiment with stripes and checks, mixed with floral prints.

FINISHED SIZE

Quilt: 63" x 77"/1.62 m x 1.98 m
Square size: 7"/18 cm

FABRIC QUANTITIES

$3^2/3$ yds/3.4 m of 45"/115 cm wide fabric for fabric 1
$1^1/4$ yds/1 m of 45"/115 cm wide fabric for fabric 2
$3^2/3$ yds/3.4 m of 45"/115 cm wide fabric for fabric 3
$3/4$ yd/180 cm of 45"/115 cm wide fabric for fabric 4

NOTIONS

polyester fiber stuffing
sewing thread
pins
sewing machine or overlocker

CUTTING

$1/2$"/6 mm seam allowances are included in the cutting instructions

1 Cut 8"/20 cm squares in the following quantities:
80 squares from fabric 1
24 squares from fabric 2
78 squares from fabric 3
16 squares from fabric 4

CONSTRUCTION

2 Place the squares of identical fabric together in pairs with right sides facing. Overlock or stitch around three sides to form the pillows, leaving the remaining side open.

3 Turn the pillows right side out and push out the corners neatly. Press them flat, pressing the seams carefully.

4 Turn in $1/2$"/1 cm on both edges of the open side of each pillow and press.

5 Place the squares in horizontal rows as directed below, working from the top left corner of the quilt and placing the open edge of each toward the top.
Row 1: 9 pillows of fabric 1.
Row 2: 1 pillow of fabric 1, 7 pillows of fabric 3, 1 pillow of fabric 1.
Row 3: 1 pillow of fabric 1, 3 pillows of fabric 3, 1 pillow of fabric 2, 3 pillows of fabric 3, 1 pillow of fabric 1.
Row 4: 1 pillow of fabric 1, 2 pillows of fabric 3, 1 pillow of fabric 2, 1 pillow of fabric 4, 1 pillow of fabric 2, 2 pillows of fabric 3, 1 pillow of fabric 1.
Row 5: 1 pillow of fabric 1, 1 pillow of fabric 3, 1 pillow of fabric 2, 1 pillow of fabric 4, 1 pillow of fabric 1, 1 pillow of fabric 4, 1 pillow of fabric 2, 1 pillow of fabric 3, 1 pillow of fabric 1.
Row 6: 1 pillow of fabric 1, 1 pillow of fabric 2, 1 pillow of fabric 4, 1 pillow of fabric 1, 1 pillow of fabric 3, 1 pillow of fabric 1, 1 pillow of fabric 4, 1 pillow of fabric 2, 1 pillow of

fabric 1.

Row 7: 1 pillow of fabric 1, 1 pillow of fabric 3, 1 pillow of fabric 2, 1 pillow of fabric 4, 1 pillow of fabric 1, 1 pillow of fabric 4, 1 pillow of fabric 2, 1 pillow of fabric 3, 1 pillow of fabric 1.

Row 8: 1 pillow of fabric 1, 2 pillows of fabric 3, 1 pillow of fabric 2, 1 pillow of fabric 4, 1 pillow of fabric 2, 2 pillows of fabric 3, 1 pillow of fabric 1.

Row 9: 1 pillow of fabric 1, 3 pillows of fabric 3, 1 pillow of fabric 2, 3 pillows of fabric 3, 1 pillow of fabric 1.

Row 10: 1 pillow of fabric 1, 7 pillows of fabric 3, 1 pillow of fabric 1.

Row 11: 9 pillows of fabric 1.

6 Butting the edges of adjoining pillows together and using a zigzag or overlock stitch, join the pillows together in rows in the correct sequence.

7 Place a small quantity of fiber stuffing in each pillow. Take care, as overstuffing will make it difficult to stitch the pillows together accurately. Pin the openings closed.

8 Butt the edges of adjoining rows together and stitch them together in the same way, closing the open side of each square as you stitch.

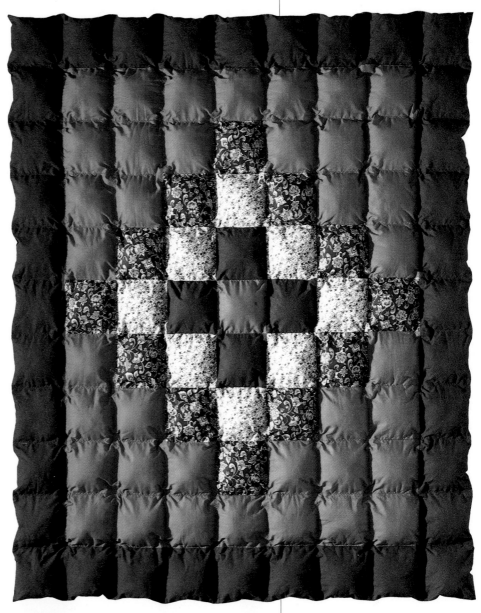

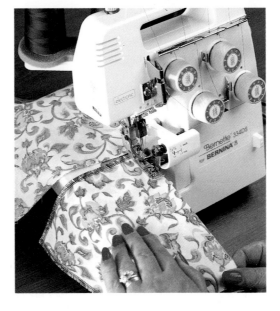

Above: The complete Pillow Quilt
Left: Joining the pillows using a Bernina overlocker

PATCHWORK NURSERY QUILT

Kate McEwen made this nursery quilt using four different but harmonising patterns in dress-weight cotton. Here we include two options for this pretty nursery quilt design. This very easy-to-sew quilt is machine-pieced and machine-quilted.

FABRIC SUGGESTIONS
Mix print and solid fabrics as well as colors, picking up some of those fabrics in some frilled curtains.

FINISHED SIZE
Quilt: 34" x 46"/82 cm x 110 cm
Block size: 6"/14 cm square
Total number of blocks: 24

FABRIC QUANTITIES
All fabrics are 45"/115 cm wide
$1/3$ yd/30 cm of cream cotton fabric
$1^2/3$ yds/1.5 m of cotton fabric for
    strips, binding and backing
$7/8$ yd/70 cm each of two other fabrics
36" x 48"/86 cm x 115 cm batting

NOTIONS
pencil and ruler
rotary (Olfa) cutter and mat
safety pins, pins and scissors
sewing machine

CUTTING
$1/2$"/1 cm seam allowances are included in the cutting instructions. Cut the backing 36" x 48"/86 cm x 115 cm before cutting the strips.

1 From each of the fabrics cut and piece a strip $2^1/2$"/6 cm wide and 5 yds/4.4 m long.

CONSTRUCTION
2 Join the four strips together lengthwise in whatever color arrangement you like, forming a strip approximately 7"/18 cm wide. Press the seams to one side.

3 Cut the strip into 7"/18 cm lengths, to make twenty-four squares.

4 Lay the squares out, in four rows of six, taking care to alternate the direction of the seams in the blocks as shown. Sew the squares into rows, then join the rows to form the quilt top. Press.

5 Measure the width of the quilt, measuring through the center. Cut two strips of the inner border fabric to this length and $2^1/2$"/6 cm wide. Sew these to the top and bottom of the quilt top. Measure the length of the quilt top, including the top and bottom borders. Cut two strips of the inner border fabric to this length and $2^1/2$"/6 cm wide. Sew these to the sides of the quilt.

6 Repeat the process in Step 5 for the outer border, cutting the fabric 4"/10 cm wide.

QUILTING
7 Place the backing fabric face down on a table. Place the batting on top and the quilt top on top of that, facing up. Pin-baste the three layers together.

8 Machine-quilt around all the blocks and borders in the seamlines.

FINISHING
9 Measure the width of the quilt as before and cut the binding fabric $2^1/2$"/6 cm wide to this length. Fold the binding strip in half lengthwise, wrong sides together. Sew the binding to the right side of the top and bottom of the quilt with raw edges even. Fold to the back and slipstitch in place. Repeat for the side bindings.

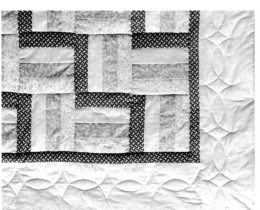

Left: A delightful
addition to any nursery
Below left: Try a slightly
different arrangement
of colors and strips
Below: Keep your baby
cozy and warm with a
special quilt

CHICKEN WALL QUILT

Strong, clear colors work best for a pictorial quilted wall hanging like this one which uses a mixture of appliqué and piecing. The black borders give the quilt great definition. Designed and made by Doffy White.

FABRIC SUGGESTIONS

Printed and plain cotton fabrics cleverly represent corrugated roofing, feathers and even eggs. The tartan binding adds a whimsical touch.

FINISHED SIZE

Quilt: 43"/107 cm square

FABRIC QUANTITIES

30"/75 cm square ticking for the background
4" x 40"/10 cm x 100 cm each four different red prints for the borders
$1^1/3$ yds/120 cm of 45"/115 cm wide black fabric for the inner borders around the roof and the outer borders
four strips tartan fabric 3 $^1/4$" x 45"/ 8 cm x 112 cm for the binding
45"/112 cm square backing fabric
a variety of scrap fabrics for feathers, eggs, chicken bodies, combs and beaks
45"/112 cm square batting

NOTIONS

13 mm wide black bias binding
sewing thread and quilting thread
pencil, tracing paper and ruler
sewing machine

CUTTING

See the pattern outlines on pages 108 and 109.
$^1/2$"/1 cm seam allowances are included in the cutting instructions unless stated otherwise.

1 Add $^1/2$"/1 cm seam allowances to all the following pieces. Cut out two chicken bodies, using the pattern outline. Cut twenty-five feathers in random sizes and shapes from the red print fabrics. Cut two chicken combs and two chicken beaks from plain fabric, following the pattern outline. Cut eight eggs from plain white fabric.

CONSTRUCTION

2 Cut four strips, each 6"/15 cm wide and 30"/75 cm long from the black fabric. Place these in pairs and, using a small jar lid, mark scallops across one long edge of each pair. Round off the space between the scallops. Stitch the strips together in pairs along the scalloped edge. Trim the seams and clip into the curves. Turn them right side out and press the scallops.

3 Cut two more black strips, each about 24"/60 cm long and 5 $^1/4$"/ 13 cm wide. Press under $^1/2$"/1 cm on one long side of each piece.

4 Open out one folded edge of the bias binding and sew this edge, right sides facing to the right side of all the feathers, bodies, beaks, eggs and combs with the raw edges matching. Note that one comb is reversed. Press the bias binding over to the wrong side, leaving a black border around all the pieces.

5 Lay the ticking background on a table and arrange the scalloped pieces at the top and bottom. Tuck the tops and bottoms of the other two black pieces underneath these scalloped pieces, placing the folded edge towards the center and angling the lower edge outwards as shown, so that it disappears altogether. Baste the black panels onto the ticking. Turn the piece over and trim the black fabric even with the ticking.

6 Position the chicken bodies as shown, tucking under the feathers, combs and beaks. Pin and baste these into place. Pin and baste the eggs into position. Machine-stitch around all the pieces, through all thicknesses.

7 Measure the width of the complete panel through the center. Cut two $3^{1}/4$"/8 cm wide borders plus seam allowances in two different red print fabrics to this length. Stitch them to the top and bottom of the panel. Measure the quilt length through the center and cut two strips, $3^{1}/4$"/8 cm wide plus seam allowances, to this length. Stitch them to both sides of the trimmed panel, enclosing the raw ends of the top and bottom borders.

8 Repeat Step 7 for the black borders, joining them to the red ones.

9 Place the backing fabric, face down on a table with the batting on top. Place the trimmed panel face up on top. Pin-baste or baste the layers together. Hand-quilt around the borders and all the edges of the appliquéd pieces. Trim off excess batting and backing fabric.

10 Cut two strips of tartan fabric to the length of the quilt and $3^{1}/4$"/8 cm wide. Making a $1^{1}/4$"/3 cm seam, sew the tartan binding to each side edge with right sides together and raw edges even. Turn in $^{1}/2$"/1 cm on remaining long edge of each strip, take the binding over to the wrong side and handsew the folded edge to the previous row of stitching. Repeat for the top and bottom edges of the quilt, folding in the raw ends.

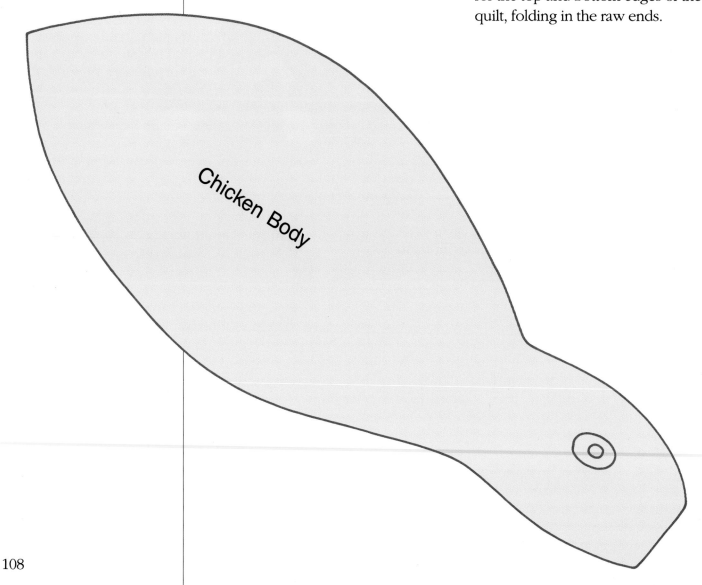

Chicken Body

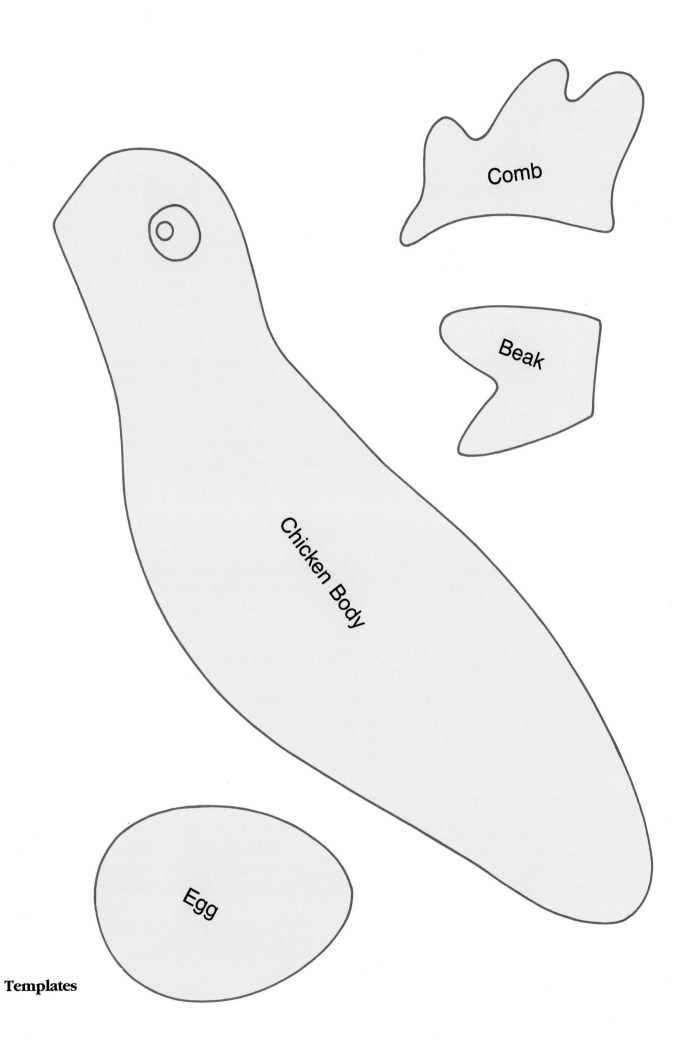

Comb

Beak

Chicken Body

Egg

Templates

QUILTED CUSHIONS

Tonia Todman designed these pieced and quilted cushions as a pair and the only difference between them is in the varying ways the colors and prints have been used. As the lines are all straight, the design is also a pleasing way to show stripes and plaid fabrics. The cushions were made by Martina Oprey.

FABRIC SUGGESTIONS

These cushions effectively combine solid and printed cotton fabrics of the same weight. They were selected from a coordinating range produced especially for patchwork.

FINISHED SIZE

16"/40 cm square, plus piping

FABRIC QUANTITIES

For each cushion:

$1/4$ yd/20 cm of 45"/115 cm wide fabric for the center square and smaller corner squares
$1/2$ yd/44 cm square for back fabric for bias piping
scrap pieces for side strips

NOTIONS

For each cushion:
cushion insert
2 yds of cotton cording for piping
$3/4$ yd fine quilter's batting
12" zipper

CUTTING

Do not forget to add $1/2$"/1 cm seam allowances to all the pieces you cut, except for the back panel which has $1/2$"/1 cm seam allowances included.

For each cushion:

1 Cut one $5^1/2$"/14 cm square for the center, four 4"/10 cm squares for the corners, four strips $1^1/4$" x 8"/3 cm x 20 cm for the inner strips A, four strips $1^1/2$" x 8"/3 cm x 20 cm for inner strips B, four strips $2^1/2$" x 8"/3 cm x 20 cm for the outer strips, two panels 17" x $9^1/2$"/42 cm x 23 cm for the cushion back.

2 Cut sufficient 2"/5 cm wide bias strips to make 2 yds/1.70 m of bias piping.

CONSTRUCTION

3 Stitch two inner strips A to either side of the center square, trimming off any excess even with the square.

4 Stitch two remaining strips A to the top and bottom of the center square, stitching over the ends of the first A strips.

5 Stitch the inner B strips to the outer strips in pairs along one long side. Stitch the B-side of one of these pairs to an A strip on one side of the center square. Stitch another one to the opposite A strip.

6 Stitch a 4"/10 cm square to each end of each remaining joined pair of strips. Center and stitch each B edge to a remaining A edge, stitching across the ends of the previously sewn-on pairs of strips. Press well.

QUILTING

7 Fold the cushion front diagonally both ways and press an X into the center panel of the cushion.

8 Pin-baste the cushion top to the fine batting. Align the edge of the presser foot or your machine's quilting guide with the creases and stitch a triangle in each quarter of the center panel. Continue making smaller triangles, using the presser foot or the quilting guide as your guide until the space is filled. Using the same technique, stitch squares in the corner squares.

FINISHING

9 Fold the bias piping strip in half, with wrong sides together, inserting the piping cord in the fold. Using the zipper foot of your sewing machine, stitch close to the cord. Trim the seam allowance to $^{1}/_{2}$"/1 cm.

10 Baste the piping to the right side of the cushion front, with raw edges even. Clip piping seam allowance at the corners for ease and finish ends neatly.

11 Place the two cushion backs together, right sides facing and raw edges matching. Stitch across one 17"/42 cm side using a 1"/2 cm seam allowance, and leaving a 12"/30 cm gap in the center for the zipper. Press the seam open. Stitch the zipper into the opening. Open zipper.

12 Place the cushion front and back together, right sides facing. Stitch around the edge of the

cushion, following the stitching line for the piping. Clip away excess fabric at corners. Turn the cushion right side out, place the cushion insert inside and close the zipper.

Below: A quilting guide on your sewing machine is useful for quilting rows
Right: A smart pair of pieced and quilted cushions

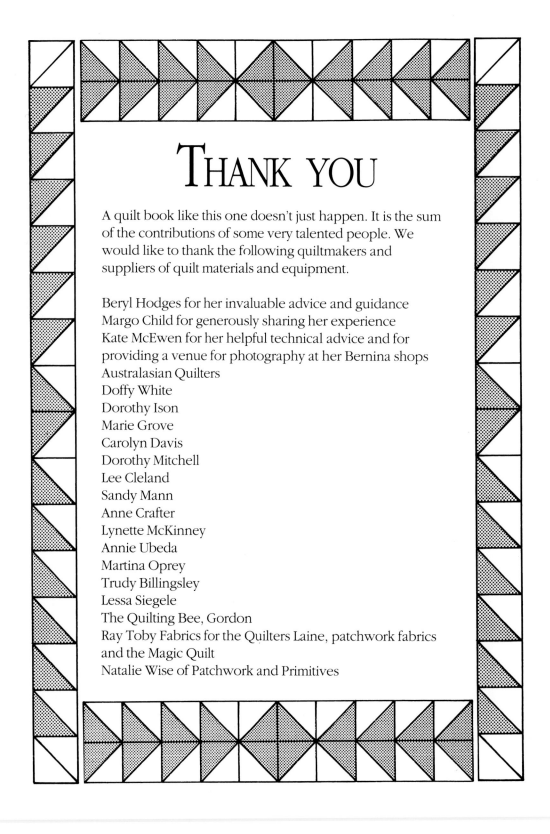

THANK YOU

A quilt book like this one doesn't just happen. It is the sum of the contributions of some very talented people. We would like to thank the following quiltmakers and suppliers of quilt materials and equipment.

Beryl Hodges for her invaluable advice and guidance
Margo Child for generously sharing her experience
Kate McEwen for her helpful technical advice and for providing a venue for photography at her Bernina shops
Australasian Quilters
Doffy White
Dorothy Ison
Marie Grove
Carolyn Davis
Dorothy Mitchell
Lee Cleland
Sandy Mann
Anne Crafter
Lynette McKinney
Annie Ubeda
Martina Oprey
Trudy Billingsley
Lessa Siegele
The Quilting Bee, Gordon
Ray Toby Fabrics for the Quilters Laine, patchwork fabrics and the Magic Quilt
Natalie Wise of Patchwork and Primitives